PRAISE FOR *ZONE GOLF*

D1516338

"*Zone Golf* is a breakthrough in golf trainin[g] aids are a dime a dozen but mind management is the next frontier for our industry, and *Zone Golf* is at the forefront of this movement. Not since *Zen Golf* was written has there been a groundbreaking approach to the game, and Kelly Sullivan Walden has given us just that. Read, learn and enjoy the game to your fullest potential."

Brian Allman, president, Sweet Spot Golf (www.sweetspotgolfclubs.com)
Santa Monica, CA
Handicap 19.5

"The exercises for self-hypnosis have not only helped my golf game, but also other areas of my life. I know now how to make my dreams come true."

Patty Collins
San Juan Capistrano, CA
Handicap 10

"I couldn't have starred in the movie *Tin Cup*. I've tried every training device. The culprit was always the club, until I read *Zone Golf*. It made me realize that what was missing from my bag was a zoned-in mind."

Doug Champagne
New Orleans, LA
Handicap 18

"Thank you *Zone Golf*, my yips have given away to a Tiger pump!"

Andrew Warburton
Temecula, CA
Handicap 11

"I see a great deal of similarity between *Zone Golf* and Timothy Gallwey's best seller *The Inner Game of Tennis*. But the difference is *Zone Golf* transforms anxieties into confidence on the course life."

Faiyaz Farouk
Cambridge, MA
Handicap 9

"I fell asleep reading your book! I'm now a believer that my inner golf critic went to sleep too!"

Jim Mitchel
Annapolis, MD
Handicap 17

"Because I'm in the entertainment world, I really related to your *Zone Golf* playlists. Now when I go to the tee box I hear 'I Believe I Can Fly,' and on the fairway Van Halen's 'Jump.' It puts me in the Zone. And I'm enjoying golf more."

Derek Partridge
Las Vegas, NV
Handicap 13

"I've played golf my whole life. I think I have read every how-to book. They all say about the same things. But not *Zone Golf.* It helps you to manage your mind and that's where the game is played."

Kermit O.
Mission Viejo, CA
Handicap 1

"If you want to lower your score and enjoy it more, then *Zone Golf* is a must-read! It made me realize that my home course resides within me! *Zone Golf* transcends golf."

John Gefrom
San Diego, CA
Handicap 8

"Extremely well written, easy to understand, concise, and at the end of the day I am able to easily implement the information into my routine. In fact, every time I review the Zone Golf Program I find it easier to focus, with the result being a continual improvement in my score. It definitely works!"

Rick Cacciatore, president, Iowa Dental Supply, Board of the Dental Trade

"In *Zone Golf*, Kelly Sullivan Walden has merged hypnosis and golfing into a hands-on practice. The eight secrets/exercises are straightforward and easy to follow and apply. This book is not only a great guide for golfers, but for anyone looking for a way to get their minds out of the sand trap and onto the green of life."

Jared Drake, director-producer of Visioneers
Topanga, CA

"I have been an athlete, student, teacher, businessman, and meditator for over thirty years…and a terrible golfer! What Kelly Sullivan Walden has done in her Zone Golf Program is a blessing. She has used the metaphor of golf as a way to live a deeper and richer life through simple and powerful truths and practices. She eloquently describes the state of grace known as 'the Zone' and teaches ways to fall into, and stay in it. She teaches that there is nothing mental about the 'Zone.' She shows how one must use the mind to get beyond the mind. As I continue to use the Zone Golf Program, I have no doubt that my golf game will continue to improve. Yet I'm far more excited about what it will do to my business and personal endeavors."

Matthew Mitchell
Santa Fe, NM
Handicap 20

ZONE GOLF

MASTER YOUR MENTAL GAME USING SELF-HYPNOSIS

KELLY SULLIVAN WALDEN

sourcebooks

Published by Sourcebooks, Inc.
P.O. Box 4410, Naperville, Illinois 60567-4410
(630) 961-3900
Fax: (630) 961-2168
www.sourcebooks.com

Library of Congress Cataloging-in-Publication Data

Walden, Kelly Sullivan.
    Zone golf : master your mental game using self-hypnosis / Kelly Sullivan Walden.
        p. cm.
    1. Golf—Psychological aspects. 2. Autogenic training. 3. Hypnotism. I. Title.
GV979.P75W33 2010
796.35201'9—dc22
                                    2009039231

Printed and bound in the United States of America.
VP 10 9 8 7 6 5 4 3 2 1

This book is dedicated to my father and hero, Frank Sullivan. Thank you for being my Golf Google and Hero. Because of you, Tiger Woods and I have something in common—our dads who first introduced us to the game.

Special thanks to Bill Fawcett, for his vision and insight, and for planting the seeds for this project many years ago.

NOTE TO READERS

As with any psychological, health, or fitness program, readers are advised to consult their physician before making any major change in their exercise or therapeutic routine.

"Inspiration comes forth from within. It's what the light burning within you is about, as opposed to motivation, which is doing it because if you don't do it, there will be negative repercussions. Motivation is making myself do something that I don't really want to do. Inspiration is having the clear picture of what I am wanting—and letting Universal forces come into play to get the outcome."

—*Abraham-Hicks*

CONTENTS

Act like you own the place

Own the course as if you were the king or queen of the green. Because golf is a game comprised of managing mistakes, rarely do even the best golfers execute a shot exactly as they see it. When you up your confidence level by acting like you own the place, whether you are teeing off or putting, the yips disappear and your natural genius emerges. (Scripts: Zone Golf Visioning and Zone Golf Goal Setting)

Turn your thinking on its head and become the master of your mind

When you master your mind, you discover your ability to neutralize your inner critic while turning up the volume of your inner champion. (Script: Mind Mastery)

ZONE Golf Secret #3—The Heart of the Matter
Let your heart do the thinking

When your heart is chaotic, so are your mind and body, with the results being jerky swings and thoughtless misses. However, when you make a "you turn" from your head to your heart, you experience entrainment, giving rise to straight shots, dropped putts, and being more of the golfer you aspire to be. (Scripts: Heart Centered)

ZONE Golf Secret #4—The *One* in *Zone*
You are connected to everything and not separate from anything

Einstein said that our separation is an optical illusion of consciousness. We perceive separation from the left hemisphere of our brain and unity from the right hemisphere. When you experience oneness on the golf course, you are accessing your right brain, which puts you in your "right" mind and releases your natural talent. This chapter will give you a quantum leap in your ability to enter into the Zone and stay there. (Scripts: Quantum Oneness and Four Elements)

ZONE Golf Secret #5—Zone In
Your natural golfing genius already resides within you

Just as the blueprint for the mighty oak tree resides within the acorn, your natural golfing genius already resides within you. This chapter will assist you in entering the Zone and connecting with your inner golf pro via music as you create your own one-of-a-kind Zone Golf soundtrack. (Scripts: Zone In and Becoming the Golf Pro You Are)

Arrive at the golf course after already playing a winning game…in your mind. If you prepare, play by play, shot by shot, imagining in detail your ideal game, you are already on your way to a winning game of golf. (Scripts: Hall of Fame, Tower of Power, and Thrive)

Every person, without exception, can transform any fragility to fortune, tragedy to triumph, and a weak golf score to one that will make him or her stand and cheer. Maximizing the accessibility of your subconscious mind in the moments before and during sleep is one of the fastest ways to improve your golf game and your life. Secret #7 is about integrating dreamwork, affirmations, and the law of attraction. This is the magic formula to bring about quantum change on and off the golf course. (Scripts: Hot Air Balloon and System Upgrade)

When you flip your passion switch, in effect, you are feeding your brain dopamine and serotonin, which stabilizes your ideal mental and emotional states. You will realize that with the strong foundation of a healthy physical and mental body, you can easily make the Zone home sweet home, or rather Zone sweet Zone. (Scripts: Passion and Star)

ACKNOWLEDGMENTS

I'd like to thank the following people for being instrumental in the creation of this book.

First and foremost, Frank Sullivan, my dad and hero, and the main inspiration for this book.

Dana Walden, my beloved husband and partner in this adventurous life of ours—thank you for your masterful recording and music that add the necessary element of magic to the Zone Golf Program.

Bill Fawcett for his vision, insight, and passion for this project—not to mention his foresight in planting the seeds for this project many years ago.

Rev. Michael Beckwith, the founder and spiritual director of Agape International Spiritual Center, for teaching me the power of vision and "visioning."

Shana Drehs, my patient and detail-oriented editor—thank God for you, for helping to smooth out the rough edges and for making this book and program sparkle.

And Gini Gentry, for providing support and the magical Garden of the Goddess retreat center as a "magical theater" backdrop in which to write this book—and for helping me to expand and elevate my mastery of awareness.

ZONE GOLF (Z-OWN IT!)

If you are like most people who will read this, you have already hired a golf instructor, taken lessons to improve your swing, purchased the latest weighted club, and perhaps even implemented golf handicap–tracker software. You may have learned all about the mental game of golf and envisioned yourself walking down the fairway with Tiger Woods after sinking a hole in one. After all that, you know the mechanics of the swing, and you understand that your mind has something to do with how well you do (or don't do) on the course. Yet you still feel that you are not playing as well as you know you are capable of playing.

Even the best players have experienced what you are feeling right now. The difference between the average-Joe golfer and someone who breaks through to a higher level is the willingness to do what it takes to make the *Zone* home sweet home (or Zone sweet Zone, as I like to call it). And that is exactly what you are beginning to do—simply by holding this book in your hands.

If you are looking for a typical golf how-to book filled with cutting-edge ideas about how to grip your putter, you may want to keep on looking. If, however, you are open to reading a book that will elevate not only your golf game but your everyday life as well, then look no further. If you are man or woman enough to set aside the rules by which you are used to playing, then this book will open the door to opportunities to lower your golf score and raise your golf experience—and your everyday life—to a level of joy. In essence, this book is not a box with hard edges and a strict, unforgiving lid but rather a spiral staircase that leads you around and around, higher and higher through mental and hypnotherapy exercises, with the result being a raised consciousness, an elevated intuition, and quickened access to the golfing mastery that awaits within you.

What Is the Zone?

Merriam-Webster's Dictionary defines *Zone* to mean "an encircling… structure," "a region or area set off as distinct from surrounding or adjoining parts," or "a temporary state of heightened concentration experienced by a performing athlete that enables peak performance [players in the *Zone*]." That sure sounds like what we're talking about!

But in order to further define what the Zone is, it might be helpful first to define what the Zone is not. And it is not any of the following: anxiousness, fear, stress, lack of confidence, worry, a self-defeating spiral, a negative self-fulfilling prophecy, or trying too hard.

Now let's talk about what the Zone is. The Zone is peace, tranquillity, ease, a lower pulse rate, a sense of focus, confidence, well-being, joy, and magnetism to the right people, places, and things. You might call it a state of grace.

This state is what Barry Sears popularized in his diet book *The Zone*. He described the Zone as peak performance during which, he claims, "your body and mind work together at their ultimate best."

On the golf course, the Zone is when you, the club, the ball, and the green are as one. The Zone is when all the things that used to distract you seem miles away. You are focused, relaxed, and yet alert, and every part of you—your mind, body, and spirit—is in sync.

Before embarking on this journey, take a moment to consider how having a consistent, reliable bridge to the Zone would affect your career, relationships, productivity, creativity, health, and overall satisfaction in life. The implications are astounding! This is what awaits you if you truly avail yourself of this program.

In this book, I will lead you on guided excursions to the innermost regions of your subconscious mind, where you will find access points to the Zone. Once inside the Zone, you will gain more control of and enjoyment in your golf game. It is important to note that the Zone is not something you can push, pull, manipulate, or force in any way. In fact, there's nothing mental about the Zone at all. Let me say that again: there is nothing mental about the Zone.

"Then how the heck is it supposed to help me with my golf game?" you might ask. And I say to you that the Zone is present once you have released all the mental clamor.

Anatomy of the Zone

There are many ways to access the Zone, some of which involve breathing techniques, yoga, meditation, and of course, reading and/or listening to the audio version of the scripts in this program.

Here are a few key points you should know about the Zone:

1. It is accessible.
2. It is constant.
3. You cannot manipulate it.
4. You must be a vibrational match to it.
5. You must combine physical practice in your golf game with your mental practice of mastering the Zone.
6. It allows your natural talent and learned golf skills to be exposed without interruption of your clamorous mind.

Don't worry—we'll address all of these in the chapters to come.

Think of the Zone as a constant stream that runs beneath the background of your mind, beneath your competitive drive to lower your score, beneath the ranting and raving because your brand-new Titleists just sank in the pond. This stream is a source of food, of electricity, of drinking water, of life, and of all that can and will make your life more satisfying and effective.

If you insist that this stream must come to you while you remain indoors, doing golf the way you've always done, then you will never benefit from its power. To access the Zone, you must go to it and dip down into it. If you have an inconsistent experience with the Zone, it is not because the Zone is whimsical; it is because you are.

The Zone is not personal. You do not have to be particularly gifted to access it, you don't have to be a math genius to be able to calculate a handicap, and you don't have to have the same $500 golf balls Tiger Woods uses. You just have to have the willingness to be an energetic match to the Zone. And that is exactly what the self-hypnosis scripts in this book are designed to help you do.

Golfing in Avalon

I liken the Zone to the mythical tale of Avalon. Avalon was an ancient place that represented a certain heaven on earth. On this isle, the Zone was a way of life. It wasn't thought of as something to attain. Harmony, joy, and peace were simply the order of the day. I'm sure if golf were played on this isle, eagles, birdies, and holes in one would have been the norm.

When people from far-off shores got wind of Avalon, they set out in droves to raid, seize, and capture it so that they could have dominion over this treasured place. But, as the tale goes, they were unsuccessful. Those in the raiding parties found themselves lost in the mist (their mental fog) that surrounded the isle, and seldom were they ever seen or heard from again. And certainly, regardless of how determined they were to stake their claim in this enchanted land, their boats never landed at Avalon's shores.

Because of this, rumors spread that Avalon disappeared altogether, and that it probably never really existed in the first place. But, as the legend goes on to say, every so often, a random fisherman, floating along in his boat, lost in the pure enjoyment of his expedition, would find his way, quite by accident, to the shores of Avalon.

The exact same principles apply to accessing the Zone. The more you try to push it or force it into place, the more it will elude you and slip right through your fingers. But if you follow the few simple principles laid out in this program, you will find yourself, like the fisherman, on Avalon's shores, in the Golf Zone. (For more about this, see Secret #1.)

Why Hypnosis?

There are many ways to access the Zone, some of which include breathing techniques, yoga, and meditation. But we're going to talk about another way, and that's hypnosis: reading and/or listening to the audio version of the self-hypnosis scripts in the Zone Golf Program.

Many professional athletes, including golfers, use some form of hypnosis or have a personal hypnotherapist with whom they consult regularly to improve and maintain peak performance—though most of them do not announce this publicly! Three of the major reasons that golfers use hypnosis to improve their performance are:

1. To relieve unnecessary stress while leaving sufficient performance edge for peak expression
2. To enhance concentration and focus
3. To practice visualization of all the moves needed to make the desired improvements to perform at their personal best

Hypnosis is one of the quickest and most powerful, effective, safe, and healthy ways to open the doors to the Zone and to effect positive and long-lasting change. Hypnosis addresses your subconscious mind, which is approximately 88 percent of your mind's power, as opposed to your conscious mind, which is approximately 12 percent of your mind's power.

You are most suggestible to positive change during the minutes that bookend your sleep (for more about this, see Secret #7). Think of your subconscious mind as a garden that receives thoughts or suggestions like seeds. Each and every time you read or listen to the Zone Golf self-hypnosis scripts before going to sleep at night, or upon awakening in the morning, you will be adding something akin to Miracle-Gro to the seeds of Zone Golf that have been planted in your mind.

If you do this, in a very short time, you will feel the roots and see the fruit of the action you are taking and the thoughts you are thinking. In other words, while your feelings about improving your golf game may be complicated, the process of changing your fundamental golf habits using hypnosis is simple. (For more on how hypnosis works, see Secret #1.)

Why Me?

It is rare to find a golf book written by a woman, much less by a woman who is a spiritual counselor. My friends have been respectfully wondering, "What the heck is a hypnotherapist and spiritual counselor who leads goddess gatherings and dream circles doing writing a golf book?"

My response (depending on my mood) is typically this: As a certified clinical hypnotherapist, I've seen it all. Over the past fifteen years I've worked with people on issues from weight loss to smoking cessation, from performance anxiety to seasickness, from overcoming fears and phobias to past life regression—and, believe it or not, I've also worked with golfers on improving their game. And I've found that the tool of hypnosis, especially for golfers, can drastically improve not only their golf game but their life as well.

The Zone Golf Program

The complete Zone Golf Program includes eight secrets to getting into your golf Zone. Each secret (chapter) comes with at least one self-hypnosis script. The CD attached to this book includes four audio tracks that accompany the corresponding scripts. For more audio tracks, please visit www.sourcebooks.com/extras/zonegolf.

Repetition Is Good: Repetition Is Good

As you read this book, you will find areas of repetitive language and exercises. Repetition is used with the tool of hypnosis to help a person anchor and align his or her goals. One more time: you can anchor and align your goals by using the tool of repetition. By hearing the same message presented in myriad ways, you will align your mind (the director of your body) to have the improved golf game you signed up for, with the by-product being an awakened life.

The Self-Hypnosis Scripts

A hypnosis script is what a hypnotherapist uses to guide a client into a transformational experience. The self-hypnosis scripts and corresponding audio program that accompany this book will help you become more familiar with your mind's ability to more positively direct the signals your brain sends to your body on and off the golf course. They will help you enhance your golf game through improved focus and physical ease. You may even find your improved golf game secondary to the enhanced feeling of well-being and self-mastery you will discover through this experience.

The beauty of the scripts in this book is that anyone can use them. You don't have to be a certified clinical hypnotherapist to reap the benefits. Self-hypnosis is an enormously empowering way to access the power of your subconscious mind (remember, it is 88 percent of your mind's power!).

Deep Asleep

Throughout this book, and especially in the self-hypnosis script sections, you will see the phrase "deep asleep." This does not imply that you are actually going to sleep, like you do at night (though you may from time to time). "Deep asleep" is code for a state of mind: a deeply pleasurable, highly suggestible experience in which your mind is more open than normal to positive suggestions regarding improving your golf game and heightening your state of well-being.

Once you get the hang of applying self-hypnosis, each and every time you read the words "deep asleep," say the words "deep asleep," or hear the words "deep asleep" (for the purpose of deepening your state of receptivity to positive suggestions about you and your golf game), you will experience a deepening of relaxation, a heightening and igniting of your imagination, and a deeper level of absorption as the information in this program is recorded within you and will have a profound and long-lasting effect.

How to Use the 28-Day Zone Golf Program

Zone Golf 28-Day Program

Day 1	Day 2	Day 3	Day 4	Day 5	Day 6	Day 7
Script 1	Practice	Script 2	Practice	Script 3	Practice	Script 4
Day 8	Day 9	Day 10	Day 11	Day 12	Day 13	Day 14
Script 5	Practice	Script 6	Practice	Script 7	Practice	Practice/Reevaluate
Day 15	Day 16	Day 17	Day 18	Day 19	Day 20	Day 21
Script 8	Practice	Script 9	Practice	Script 10	Practice	Script 11
Day 22	Day 23	Day 24	Day 25	Day 26	Day 27	Day 28
Script 12	Practice	Script 13	Practice	Script 14	Practice	Practice/Reevaluate

Studies show that it takes 28 days to change a habit. The 28-day Zone Golf Program with its self-hypnosis scripts and audio tracks is geared to assist you in a stairstep approach to build new habits and establish a way of thinking that puts you in the optimum state for accessing the Zone in your golf game.

When to Listen: Morning or Evening

You may be wondering when the best time is to listen to these tracks: morning or evening. The answer is that both are effective, in different ways. Listening at night has more of an effect on your subconscious, and listening in the morning, in my experience, will affect you on both an unconscious and a conscious level. Listening in the morning tends to create awareness in listeners of the mind shift they are making and to set a deliberate theme for the day.

Sleep Your Way to Success

One way to increase the effectiveness of these tracks is to use them before you go to sleep. Download the additional tracks at www .sourcebooks.com/extras/zonegolf. In addition to listening to a track every other day, for reinforcement listen to track 3 on the accompanying CD and track 14 on the website as you go to sleep in the evening prior to a game day.

Practice Makes Perfect

Designate every other day (the days that you are not listening to a self-hypnosis track) as a "practice" day in which you re-create the self-hypnosis experience without the aid of reading the script in the book or listening to the audio.

During your practice days, set aside 10 to 20 minutes to relax, close your eyes, and envision the images, sensations, and positive feelings that the audio track stimulated in you on the previous day. Doing this will assist you in reinforcing your experience of the information in each track and in deepening your access to the Zone.

Take your inner work to the golf course and hit a bucket of balls or play a low-pressure round of golf as often as possible (at least once or twice a week throughout this program).

R&R Every 14 Days

Give yourself a reevaluate and readjust (R&R) day at the midpoint and at the end of your 28-day program. On these days, don't play golf and do not listen to the self-hypnosis program. Simply let these be rest days in which, if you like, you can take 10 to 15 minutes to reevaluate the goals that you set for yourself at the onset of the program. (See Secret #1.)

If you choose to review your goals, identify your progress, highlight the goals you have accomplished, and target specific areas that still need work. This will help you effectively readjust your goals for the next 14-day segment. By the time you have reached your second 14-day segment, this will bring you to the 28-day program.

Post-28-Day Program

Once you've completed the 28-day Zone Golf Program, take inventory of your goals as well as the overall way that you are playing, thinking, and feeling on the golf course.

You can now use the recordings and scripts in this book to revisit and reinforce the mental habits you are learning on an as-needed basis. A few ideas on how to do that follow:

- Pick your favorite self-hypnosis track with which to practice.
- Read the sections in the book and listen to the tracks that are the most stimulating and pleasing to you as often as you'd like. This process will assist you in deepening the positive mental grooves that you are establishing.
- Listen to the tracks that were the most challenging for you. As you do this, over time you will discover blind-spot breakthroughs, which can be (in many cases) even more profound than the transformation you will gain from the tracks that are the most resonant and enjoyable to experience.

How to Get the Maximum Benefit from Self-Hypnosis

You can experience the self-hypnosis scripts in the following four ways, depending upon what works best for you:

1. Download each script from www.sourcebooks.com/extras/zonegolf to your MP3 player.
2. Play the audio CD that accompanies this book (to listen to 4 of the 16 self-hypnosis scripts.)
3. Record each script into your own recording device and listen back to the self-hypnosis script in your own voice.
4. Read each script to yourself (silently or aloud).

Here are some tips to keep in mind when you're listening to the scripts:

- Listen to the self-hypnosis tracks when you are in a completely relaxed environment. Refrain from listening to the self-hypnosis tracks while driving, working on the computer, using sports equipment, or multitasking. Give your entire attention over to the mental practice this program provides.
- When listening to the audio portion of this program, make sure that your clothes are comfortable; your shoes are removed; and your hands, arms, and legs are uncrossed (uncrossed legs expedite relaxation and energy flow).
- Allow yourself the opportunity to listen without any distraction or any chance of distraction (e.g., unplug phones, turn the ringer down on your BlackBerry, put a Do Not Disturb sign on the door).
- Should an emergency arise at any time while listening to this program, you can get up and take care of the situation, simply by counting yourself up from zero to five (zero represents deep asleep, and five represents being wide awake, completely alert, and aware). But this would be necessary only if you went into an extremely deep state of self-hypnosis.
- As mentioned earlier, the ideal time to listen to this program is either first thing in the morning or in the evening before you drift off to sleep. These are times when your body and mind are most naturally suggestible and receptive to the positive information that can create long-lasting results.

Once you have read and/or listened to the self-hypnosis scripts laid out for you in this book, entering the Zone will become as simple as

- closing your eyes ("zoning in")
- taking three deep breaths to focus your attention on the area around your heart as you breathe in and out
- imagining the mental images and feelings associated with your picture of golf success
- forgetting everything that you've been practicing
- enjoying yourself as you play ("zoning out")

Postscript for the Rebels

Although I highly suggest that you take on the 28-day program as outlined, I am aware of the rebels in the crowd (am I talking to you?) who will want to do this program their way. I happen to be one of those people. So this is for you. Each one of these 16 self-hypnosis scripts is complete in and of itself. All of them are effective, and yet one strategy might strike a chord in you as deeper and more personal than another. You have my permission and my blessing (not that you need it) to sample from this smorgasbord in any order, at any time you'd like. The key to your success is that the program makes sense to you and resonates with the unique way that you are coded. Trust yourself, dive in, and enjoy the process (and your results!).

Oh, and Don't Forget to Practice on the Course

I assume that you are already doing many of the physical activities that one must do to become a great golfer, such as practicing your putting and swinging with a coach or golf pro. According to H. Halvari and the Sport Completion Anxiety Test, athletes who practice mental imagery show substantial enhancement to their muscle strength, movement dynamics, and motor-skill performance. This test and many like it show that physical practice combined with mental practice is an unbeatable combination.

In other words, to gain maximum effectiveness from this program, do yourself the favor of combining physical practice with a golf pro along with your Zone practice (reading and listening to the self-hypnosis scripts offered in this book).

Major Change Comes Down to One Word: *Decision*

Some people, upon reading this book and listening to the accompanying audio tracks, will dramatically improve their golf game. The difference between someone whose golf game is dramatically changed by this program and someone whose life is just slightly improved is a decision to take in the information, deeply experience the self-hypnosis scripts, and suspend the disbelief that radical transformation in your golf game is possible, probable, and attainable. If you decide that this is it, the definitive moment when you step out of your history and into the mystery of being the golfer you've only dared to dream of being, then the moment of dramatic improvement has arrived.

Your mind is extremely powerful. With your mind you create worlds. With your mind you can turn the invisible into the visible. And with your mind you can transform the illogical into the logical. This book is about taking what you have been dreaming about and making it happen.

Expect the best—change has already begun! Enjoy!

WHY HYPNOSIS IS NOT A BUNCH OF HOOEY

Skeptics Stop Here!

If you are reading this with a sideways glance, either because you are new to the concept of self-hypnosis or because it just seems too airy-fairy for your rational disposition, then this section is for you. I have found in my years of working with clients that it is necessary to demystify hypnosis while offering an understanding of its nuts and bolts so that they can relax and enjoy the process. To do that, here I outline the fundamentals of hypnosis, self-hypnosis, the alpha state, and how all of those things work together to help you drastically improve your golf game.

If hypnosis is old hat to you and you just want to sink your teeth into the self-hypnosis scripts, then feel free to skip ahead to Secret #1 or to enjoy this section as a reinforcement of what you may already know.

If you are new to self-hypnosis or are curious but have your reservations, then this section will be helpful to you in that it offers a grounding in what hypnosis actually is and how it can greatly assist you on the course.

Although I cannot guarantee that by reading this and listening to the corresponding audio tracks that you will become the next Tiger Woods, I can guarantee that by participating in this program, you will become more fluent in the Zone (on and off the golf course).

The remainder of this chapter should answer most of your questions, and I hope you will come to an understanding that the self-hypnosis process is one that will serve only to enhance the physical work you are already doing in your golf lessons and practice sessions to increase your enjoyment of the game.

What Is the Difference between Hypnosis and Self-Hypnosis?

All hypnosis is self-hypnosis.

When clients come to see me, I tell them, "I am not going to do something to you. I am not a genie in a bottle who is going to change your handicap with a nod of the head and a wink of an eye. You are in control of your life, and you are the one and only one who has the power to accept or reject suggestions or impressions that come your way."

As a certified clinical hypnotherapist, I am essentially a coach. I train people to get out of their own way and use their minds in an empowering way. I train people to dehypnotize themselves from the false and limited belief systems they have accumulated over the years in order to uncover their natural genius that has always been there, just beneath the surface.

I tell my clients that the work we do in my office is a springboard to set change in motion. The work we do together is a catalyst, a pep rally, an empowerment blast that initiates you powerfully in the direction you desire to go. However, the dramatic transformation comes from your willingness to participate in your own evolution by continuing the work that we begin, in your own life, on and off the golf course. The radical change that is possible with hypnotherapy comes from your use of the tool of hypnosis to change the environment in your mind. And those tools are contained in the book that you are now holding in your hand.

But to get more specific, self-hypnosis is actually the art of being able to access a hypnotic state intentionally on your own, without a hypnotherapist in your physical proximity to guide you.

Suggestibility: Is Everyone Hypnotizable?

People often ask me if everyone can be hypnotized. This is a valid question, given that there are so many misconceptions surrounding hypnotism. Not only do many people question the universality of hypnosis, but also some professional hypnotists and hypnotherapists today believe that only a percentage of people can be hypnotized. The bottom line, in my experience, is that everyone is hypnotizable; however, some are more naturally suggestible than others, and some are more resistant than others.

Perhaps two of the reasons people believe that only some folks are hypnotizable are the popular hypnotizability scales put forth by Stanford University (created in 1959) and Harvard University (created in 1962). The researchers for these scales concluded that, although 95 percent of people are hypnotizable, 5 percent of people cannot be hypnotized. On the basis of my clinical experience, I agree with these studies, in that I know there are those (let's call them the control freaks) who find it difficult to near impossible to release their stranglehold on life. However, in my experience, I have seen that even the most tightly wound individuals, if they dedicate themselves to unraveling their rigidity (through meditation, yoga, and/or dreamwork) can find themselves able to enjoy the opportunity that hypnosis provides them. So, if you fall into this category, don't give up hope. The fact that you are reading this book now is a demonstration of your willingness to expand. Remember, 50 percent of change is a sincere desire to do so—you are halfway there!

Hypnotic Phenomena

All sorts of hypnotic phenomena occur naturally, to everyone. These include visual hallucinations, hypnotic anesthesia, time distortion, and amnesia. As you familiarize yourself with these examples, you will see how these apply to your life and your golf game. In so doing, your mind may open to consider the possibility that all people are hypnotizable.

For example, everyone has experienced the hypnotic phenomena known as visual hallucinations, whereby you see what you expect to see (or to not see, as the case may be). Visual hallucinations can be positive or negative. For instance, if you have ever held a bottle of champagne but envisioned that it was the Stanley Cup, that is an example of a positive hallucination. If you have ever driven the golf ball into a tree that you didn't notice was blocking your shot, your failure to see the tree is a negative hallucination. Hypnotic anesthesia is occurring when, say, you have a terrible headache and a friend makes a funny joke to distract your mind away from the pain, or maybe when you watch Tiger Woods make one of his jaw-dropping putts and for a while feel completely free of discomfort. During hypnotic anesthesia, you are completely unaware of any sensations in your body. As John Parziale, MD, told the *American Journal of Physical Medicine and Rehabilitation*, 80 percent of golfers report having pains, illness, or injuries, and 27 percent have back problems. So, becoming aware of the ways you can use hypnotic anesthesia might prove helpful to you in your golf game as well as in your life.

If you have experienced time passing more slowly or more quickly than the actual movement of the hands on your watch, then you have experienced the hypnotic phenomena called time distortion. We have all had experiences when time has seemed to drag or to fly. If you are waiting in line behind a duffer for your turn to tee off, it may seem that five minutes has stretched into eternity. In contrast, when you're in the Zone, playing your best and sinking putts from improbable distances, you may get to your eighteenth hole only to have it seem that you arrived at the course just a few minutes before. Where did the time go?

Hypnotic amnesia is when your senses become overloaded and you block out what is happening around you. For example, let's say your golf pro is giving you tips on your swing. Out of the corner of your eye, you see a golfer who is older and more out of shape than you drive the ball 350 yards, and suddenly you have no recollection of what your pro just told you. You tell him, "Would you please repeat that? My mind was somewhere else."

After reading this, you will no doubt begin to notice the way hypnotic phenomena weave their way naturally and frequently throughout your daily life, in both your mundane and your peak experiences. One thing that all these different forms of hypnotic phenomena have in common is that they all involve mental distraction. Your body may be doing one thing, like gripping your club, but your mind is thinking of something else. If you are mentally elsewhere, you are by definition not aware of what is happening with your body, and thus you open yourself to experience all sorts of hypnotic phenomena.

There are many more hypnotic phenomena, but the point I want to make is that hypnosis is not a foreign experience to be feared and resisted. It is a natural and normal part of your life that, with awareness, can be of great benefit as you endeavor to make positive changes to your life and your golf game.

The term *hypnosis* is simply a state of mind in which the drawbridge to your subconscious is down long enough that ideas from the outside can enter the castle of your mind.

Your Imagic-nation

You know already that hypnosis occurs naturally, but now we're going to talk about how you can harness it to work for you.

Hypnosis comes from your imagination, and your imagination creates magic—that is why it is actually your "imagic-nation." You can accomplish great things with your own mind.

For example, when you took your first golf lesson, while your instructor was showing you how to grip your nine iron, you may have been imagining what it would be like to swing like Arnold Palmer. This imagining process may seem simple, but it actually serves many purposes. It opens your mind to an experience of learning that hastens the road to mastery. It stimulates you by activating a greater degree of your brain function, and it entertains you, which increases endorphins and gives you an overall sense of health and well-being.

If you pretend to be Jack Nicklaus while you are whacking a bucket of balls or act as if you were Annika Sorenstam while sizing up your next shot, you are in effect practicing self-hypnosis. What you put your attention on and imagine with detail must reveal results in your golf game.

Can you recall a time when you were reading a great book, watching a dramatic scene in a movie, or engaging in a deep conversation and the external world faded from your awareness? All it truly takes to use self-hypnosis is to engage your imagic-nation by layering your senses: visual, auditory, or kinesthetic. The bottom line is that we human beings are all suggestible. We all are affected by the stimuli around us. The name of the game is to have mastery over our awareness so that we can be deeply suggestible when it serves us to be and not suggestible when it does not serve us to be.

Some people pride themselves on how unhypnotizable they are, as if to say that they are not gullible. This is a fantastic skill if someone is trying to sell you a pet rock as a golf good-luck charm. It is great to be discerning. But think of your suggestibility like a light switch. You want to be able to turn it on and off at will.

The Gods Must Be Crazy

The word *hypnosis* comes from the Greek word for "sleep." In Greek mythology, Hypnos was the god of sleep who lived in perpetual darkness and mist in an underground cavern. His water supply was the river Lethe (forgetfulness), of course, which flowed through his underground lair. Hypnos is depicted as spending his days either lounging on a couch surrounded by his many sons, the Oneiroi (which means "dreams"), or intervening in the lives of mortals through their dreams and visions.

According to an article on the history of hypnosis by Wil Dieck, in 1843, the Scottish surgeon James Braid coined the term *hypnosis*, inspired by his knowledge of Hypnos. In his dissertation, "Neurypnology Or The Rationale Of Nervous Sleep: Considered In Relation With Animal Magnetism," Braid described hypnotism as the science of inducing trance. Thanks to Braid's introduction of the word *hypnosis*, it is now commonly known as an altered state of awareness. And, as mentioned previously, contrary to popular understanding, hypnosis or trance is a naturally occurring state. In fact, we all enter this state several times every single day of our lives, such as when we are watching television; reading books, newspapers, or magazines; driving home from work; taking a shower; brushing our teeth; preparing for sleep; or lining up our putter. Hypnosis is a perfectly safe and natural state of mind in which we are in deeper communion with our subconscious mind than we are when we are in a more linear, cerebral state of being.

Hypnotherapy versus Conscious-Level Therapy

Hypnosis works with your imagination at the level of the subconscious mind, where your core beliefs, values, emotions, and memories of past events reside. According to the Hypnosis Motivation Institute, traditional cognitive therapies work with your willpower at the level of the conscious mind (which accounts for 12 percent of your mind's power), whereas hypnosis works with you on the level of your subconscious mind (which accounts for 88 percent of your mind's power). So, hypnosis can assist you in accelerating your ability to imprint new mental images of yourself as a great golfer so that you'll see results in days, weeks, or months rather than the years that conscious-mind changes would take.

According to the American Hypnosis Association, hypnosis is a relaxing therapeutic experience that can be used to treat and improve issues such as the following:

- weight control
- smoking cessation
- anxiety, phobias, and panic attacks
- relationship issues
- depression
- pain management
- sleeping disorders
- bereavement counseling
- confidence
- fear of dentistry
- gambling
- alcohol dependency
- nail biting
- sports (i.e., *golf*!)

Think of what it would be like to be the golfer you always knew you could be. Of course, the perfect recipe for change is plenty of physical practice combined with the mental conditioning of self-hypnosis. Like clay, you will literally mold yourself into the best golfer you are capable of becoming.

A Meeting of the Minds

The only way to create radical change and transformation is to have both the conscious and subconscious mind align in agreement to do things differently. Until our subconscious mind recognizes and receives our conscious desire, our two minds will remain in conflict and our progress will be slow and tedious. But when the conscious and subconscious minds agree, the conscious desire becomes subconscious action. At this point, the inner tug-of-war ceases, and what we think we want to do becomes what we actually do automatically, naturally, and easily.

This is why using traditional talk therapy alone to address sports performance rarely works. Although talk therapy is extremely valuable, using it to help clients to consciously understand why they have a habit and why that habit is getting in the way of the perfect straight swing shot does not speak to or change the subconscious mind in a rapid way.

The key, therefore, to changing any unwanted habit or to transforming your golf game—from getting rid of the yips on the green to straightening out your slice at your tee off—is to rewire the subconscious mind to agree with the conscious mind's desire. Both sides of your mind have to agree to create a truly winning formula.

Exploring the Alpha State

Understanding and laying claim to the territory within you known as the Zone would be incomplete without an understanding of the alpha state.

In 1971, Dr. Herbert Benson and a team of researchers at Harvard University documented the relaxation response. The relaxation response, another term for the alpha state, is the opposite of the stressful fight-or-flight response, a state that can be induced simply by focusing on breathing. The relaxation response, or alpha state, was shown to decrease blood pressure by slowing brain waves, as well as to relieve chronic pain and to assist people with the ability to handle stress.

In the alpha state, put simply, our brains cycle at a rate of 8 to 14 times per second, which is slower than the rate we normally operate at in the hustle and bustle of our daily lives but faster than the rate at which we cycle when we are sleeping. In the alpha state, we experience a decreased heart rate and a feeling of being centered and peaceful. We feel an enhanced well-being in this state because our body's levels of cortisol (stress hormones) drop as our serotonin (well-being producing hormones) levels rise. For example, some people report having their best ideas in the shower, driving in their car, or walking along a beautifully manicured fairway. These instances, and others like them, tend to occur because people are simply relaxed and in a state of ease, and in this state, they are receptive to ideas that they would otherwise skip right over. These are examples that resemble the nature of alpha state moments, when you access higher aspects of natural thought processes.

Think of the alpha state as your mode of transportation, the boat that carries you down a lazy river. And hypnosis and hypnotherapy are the data you collect along your journey downstream that alter the way you think, feel, and golf. According to the Biocybernaut Institute, the alpha state's "aware relaxation" can induce the following:

- Calming your body and relaxing your mind while you remain alert enough to swing a golf club without hitting your fellow golfers

- Stimulating imagination, intuition, and higher awareness, which lead to an acceleration in your ability to set goals and vibrationally align with them
- Creating detachment from the outcome and increasing accuracy, which allow you to enjoy your game
- Improving concentration, decision making, and memory
- Allowing you to sleep better, fall asleep easily, and stay asleep through the night
- Keeping you healthier and even extending your longevity

What is wonderful about the alpha state is that it is a highly functional state. Unlike the beta state, which is a state of being in which your heart rate is faster, your breathing is shallower, and your thoughts tend toward the mundane and superficial (bada bing bada boom, time is money, money is time), the alpha state is productive without you having to be a stressed-out chicken running around without a head. My father used to tell me when I was younger and in a perpetual beta state, "The hurrier you go, the behinder you get!" Isn't it true? But in the alpha state, you can truly do less and accomplish more.

And as opposed to other states, such as the theta state (a highly relaxed state, as on the brink of sleep) and delta state (sleeping), mastery of the alpha state actually simultaneously relaxes you and attunes you to your inner wisdom, higher guidance, and deeper feelings, all while you're alert enough to operate a motor vehicle, heavy machinery, and a golf cart.

The best news about the alpha state, beyond its ability to lessen physical ailments, to enhance sports performance, and to bridge your conscious and subconscious minds, is that it is highly accessible.

As you read the scripts and listen to the audio tracks in the Zone Golf Program, you will start creating the alpha state as your natural set point—a regular, habitual place that sets the tone for every day of your life and every golf game you play.

Get Out There

At this point, you have an understanding of the alpha state, hypnosis, self-hypnosis, suggestibility, and why and how hypnosis can improve your golf game (as well as your mental game), and you have the recommended structure for applying the Zone Golf Program. The last thing: go forth and enjoy yourself! As I'm sure you've already experienced, when you are having fun, you tend to open the fairway of your heart and soul to your best playing. Take pleasure in the messages you'll find in each page of the following chapters—and enjoy your game!

Z-OWN IT!

Act like you own the place

Until one is committed, there is hesitancy, the chance to draw back…
Whatever you can do or dream you can. Begin it. Boldness has genius,
power, and magic in it. Begin it now.

—Goethe

Secret Synopsis

Own the course as if you were the king or queen of the green. Because golf is a game of managing mistakes, rarely do even the best golfers execute a shot exactly as they see it. When you up your confidence level by acting like you own the place, whether you are teeing off or putting, the yips disappear and your natural genius emerges.

You can read this book in two ways. One way is to read it passively, as if it were a novel, with the action taking place outside of you. The other way is to read it from the inside out—which I highly recommend—so that you participate in the book, treat it like it is alive, animated, your very own personal golf coach assisting you on a transformational journey. The way we do any one thing will show us how we approach our entire life.

In the Zone Golf Program, you will be reconfiguring not only your golf game but also the very center of your life. Your center is the source of your security, guidance, wisdom, and power. When you make a significant change in one area, it will have an impact on everything else in your life.

Take a cue from Steven Covey, the author of *The 7 Habits of Highly Effective People*, and begin with the end in mind. When you begin with the end in mind, you are transported from a myopic, ground-level point of view to the mountaintop, where you can see the entire vista. When you begin with the end in mind, all becomes clear, and you can more easily identify that which you truly desire to create. As you embark on your Zone Golf Program with the end in mind, you have a personal direction to guide your golf game, without which little can be accomplished.

Covey says, "All things are created twice. You create them first in your mind, and then you work to bring them into physical existence." By taking control of your own first creation, you can write or rewrite your scripts, and thus take control and responsibility for the outcome.

All of this might seem grandiose if you simply picked up this book for some quick and easy tips about how to shave a couple of strokes off your golf game. However, it is my belief that people who are drawn to this book might indeed want to improve their golf game, but on a much deeper level, they might desire personal transformation as well.

Zone Golf Visioning

Our deepest fear is not that we are inadequate. Our deepest fear is that we are powerful beyond measure. It is our light, not our darkness that most frightens us…And as we let our own light shine, we unconsciously give other people permission to do the same. As we are liberated from our own fear, our presence automatically liberates others.

—*Marianne Williamson*

As you embark on your Zone Golf experience, you'll want to let go of your preconceived ideas of what it is you want to accomplish. In other words, lose your mind to win the game (for more on this, see Secret #2). Losing your mind is not about going brain dead but quite the opposite. It is about uploading a higher-grade operating system than the one you're currently running.

We're going to start the process with visioning. The images, sensations, and guidance you uncover during visioning are always bigger, better, and more authentic than what you would have conjured with your own will alone.

Once you gain clarity through the visioning process, you will have a new image or vision of what you are moving toward.

What's the Difference between Visualization and Visioning?

Through visualization, we are able to mentally perceive that which we seek to manifest in our lives. For example, we can say, "I want to win the tournament tomorrow," and because our minds are powerful, we can actually create this exact experience through our mental intention and attention.

However, through visioning, we open ourselves up to even greater possibilities because we remove our human desires and allow for something greater to inform us. As we open ourselves to our greatest possibilities, we set aside our small agenda and desires, which are often based in selfish wants that limit the creation process. As we open up to the greatest vision of our life, relationships, employment, health, and golf game, we cocreate experiences that are greater than our surface mind can fathom. For example, a vision-based intent might be, "I see myself golfing at my ultimate potential."

When you enter the visioning process, you connect with a stream of information that is higher than your small, personal self. This higher stream of information is both waiting and seeking your awareness of it. Something magnificent happens when you commune in the space of allowing this stream to inform you.

Once the vision becomes clear, then take the action it inspires. When you remain open, you will be delighted as the manifestation of your vision begins to appear and gracefully unfold in your life.

As I've said, because the mind is very powerful, what you set your mind to will come to pass in one way or another.

Of course, there is a time lapse between a desire and its manifestation. Most people bemoan the buffer time, as if it hindered them from what they want. I see the buffer time as a period of time in which you become prepared to handle that which you seek. The buffer time is also a blessing that gives you the opportunity to make sure what you say you want is actually what you truly want, before you manifest it in your life.

Be Careful of What You Ask For

Have you ever gotten what you said you want (e.g., a relationship, a house, a job) only to realize that it wasn't really what you wanted? When this happens, you have to spend a lot of your creative time and energy trying to get rid of the thing you thought you wanted. With the buffer time between the visioning process and the outcomes in your life, you can evaluate and reevaluate what it is you truly want, allowing you the opportunity to align your thoughts, identity, and inner reference point with the goal you desire. This way you actually want what you are preparing to receive.

The Zone Golf Visioning Process—Bringing the Best You to the Golf Course

The Zone Golf visioning process is similar to traditional goal setting (which we will explore next) in many ways. However, there is one main difference. With traditional goal setting, you identify something you want (e.g., a lower handicap) and seek to capture it, like a carrot dangling above that you want to grasp. In the Zone Golf visioning process, you are not seeking something outside of you to become a better golfer— not a better club; fancier, high-compression 1,000-dimple golf balls, or the latest robotically plasma-welded driver. In the Zone Golf visioning process, you begin with the premise that you already have all that you need and are simply allowing something from within you to emerge.

Just as there is an oak tree within an acorn, there is a great golfer within you. And when the conditions are right (with physical and mental practice), this being within you will emerge and grow to its greatest capability.

The Zone Golf visioning process lets you release your preconceived notions to begin with as blank a canvas as you possibly can. The blank canvas erases your shoulds, resignation, doubts, cynicism, and expectations so that you can avail yourself of something new, something relevant for this brand-new moment, not last year's moment or yesterday's moment or someone else's moment, but your now moment, as distinct from any other moment, past or future.

You are an ever-changing being. Science shows that our cells renew at astounding rates and that, from year to year, we are made new. The only reason we appear the same year after year, day after day, moment after moment, with the same golf score (perhaps improving incrementally) is because our mental habits don't change. If you change your mind, you'll change your golf game, and thus you will change your life.

Preparing for the Zone Golf Visioning Process

What if you are your very own best golf pro? What if in this very instant you already have everything you need to be the best golfer you can possibly be? If you ask sincerely, you will be sincerely answered, and the answers might just blow your mind.

As you enter into the Zone Golf visioning process, you will be asked a series of questions and several minutes of silence will follow each one. This self-hypnosis program is the most interactive of all the other self-hypnosis scripts in this book in that it consists primarily of questions and blank space for your own wisdom to bubble up to the surface.

I suggest embarking on the visioning journey with pen and paper in hand. Some of the most life-changing, golf-transforming insights come from the visioning process, so do yourself the favor of not taking anything for granted and of taking careful notes.

In the upcoming Zone Golf visioning script (p. 23), you will be asked to contemplate the following questions:

- *From the highest place, what am I capable of with regard to my golf game?* Your job is simply to remain receptive and open to gaining a glimpse of your greatest possibility as a golfer, regardless of what you have previously been taught, regardless of what anyone has ever said about you, and regardless of what you have previously thought about yourself or experienced.

  Don't worry if nothing comes to mind or if something comes to mind and it seems strange to you. When you open up in this visioning self-hypnosis experience, you truly avail yourself of ideas and concepts that previously may have never entered your mind. Your job is to simply allow the insight to come to you in the unique way that you receive insight. Some people receive their insight days later, some receive insight in their dreams, some feel or hear specific words or feelings, and some imagine newspaper headlines in their minds. Do not judge your process. The fact that you are open and willing and are creating a space for the insights to come means that they will indeed come, in their own mysterious way.

- *What must I release to be in league with this vision?*

  You may become aware of a certain posture (e.g., slouched shoulders), condescending remarks you frequently make about yourself, or a particular person you spend time with who is discouraging. Don't worry about having to change your whole life right away. Simply become aware of the thoughts, beliefs, and habits that stand in the way of you revealing the golf masterpiece that you are.

- *What must I embrace?*

  Rev. Michael Beckwith says, "Pain pushes until inspiration pulls." What is inspiration guiding you to do, create, or become to put yourself into harmony with the vibration of the greatest golfer and human being that you can possibly be? Don't be alarmed. At this point, simply begin to become aware of changes that need to take place. Your awareness is like a seed that is being planted. Change will follow if you plant the seed properly.

- *What specific action steps must I take?*

  It might become clear after contemplating these questions what specific action steps you can take now. If they are not clear, then simply rest in the question and allow the answers to come to you in their time. If you remain open and receptive, you will be pleasantly surprised at the insights that will be revealed to you.

  The answer to this question may be as simple as writing down the vision from the first question and placing it in your car, wallet, or refrigerator, somewhere that you will see it each day. Or it may be working with the new golf pro at your local golf course. It may be finding a picture in a golf magazine that matches your vision and that you put in a place where you can see it before you go to sleep. Whatever it is, this final step will make the difference between your vision being a concept, a pie-in-the-sky fantasy, and a reality that is tethered to earth, one that you make progress toward every day.

Zone Golf Visioning Self-Hypnosis Script

Your Zone Golf Hypnosis Journey

Sit in a comfortable, quiet position, or recline with your head slightly elevated.

Uncross your arms and legs, and rest your hands, palms up, either by your sides or on your thighs.

Should an emergency arise at any time while in self-hypnosis, you can get up to take care of the situation simply by counting yourself up from zero to five. At five you will be wide awake, completely alert, and aware.

Close your eyes and nod your head slightly, signaling to your subconscious mind that you are ready to enter a deep state of self-hypnosis to radically improve your golf game.

As you begin, take a few very deep breaths, and you may begin to notice certain parts of your body relaxing. Perhaps other parts are still a little tense. Just become aware of this, as your body continues to relax— the way your clothes feel on your body, the way the air feels as it gently brushes up against your face.

Notice your body being completely supported by the weight of the chair, couch, bed, or whatever it is that is holding you up.

As you read this, become aware of how good it feels to breathe in deeply and slowly, and to release completely. Feel your chest and stomach rise with each inhalation, and contract with each exhalation. Notice the release and the letting go that takes place now. With each breath that you exhale, you release all your cares of the day.

With each breath you breathe out, you let go of any and all tension that may linger in your body. And with each and every inhalation, you breathe in a sense of peace and relaxation.

Begin to count yourself down into a deeper state of relaxation. Start with five and move down to zero. At zero you will go deep asleep, a receptive state of focused relaxation. And with each count, you become more and more relaxed, and completely peaceful.

Begin with five, as you let go with each breath.

Four—all tension washes away.

Three—allow yourself to feel heavy in the chair or on whatever surface holds you up.

Two—let go more than before, as you prepare yourself to discover an inner resourcefulness that will improve the way you approach your golf game and relate to yourself as a golfer.

One—prepare to enter the Zone.

Zero—deep asleep. Each and every time you read or hear "deep asleep," you go quickly, soundly, and deeply to this depth or deeper for the purpose of entering the Zone and radically transforming your mental golf game.

As you rest in deep asleep, scroll back through your memories to a place and time when you felt unconditionally loved. Loved not because you did something, not because you won a prize or impressed someone with your skills, but simply because you were being you. You might consider a time in your childhood when you felt safe, protected, and deeply cared for. This might be a moment of snuggling with your first pet or perhaps a moment from your recent past, such as feeling unconditionally loved by your partner or your child. Just notice how this feeling opens you, and allow it to permeate your being.

Once you steep for a few minutes in the quality of unconditional love, you are primed and ready to contemplate the following questions.

From the highest place, what am I capable of with regard to my golf game?

- What is the feeling vibration?
- What does it look like?
- What does it sound like?
- What does it taste or smell like?
- What are the qualities of my highest expression of the golfer I am capable of being?

Allow yourself time to ruminate with these questions.

Drop any preconceived notions about what you think you should look like, feel like, sound like, or be like as the golfer you are capable of becoming. Simply remain receptive and open to glimpsing your highest possibility as a golfer. Give yourself full permission to simply envision the largess of who and what you are capable of being.

Take a couple of deep breaths as you allow this vision to sink in. (Allow yourself a few moments to integrate the new information.)

With this next breath, open yourself to the next questions:

- What must I release to be in league with this vision?
- What must I let go of to be a space that can contain this vision?
- What habits must I transform?
- Is there something I am doing, eating, or spending time on that is in the way of my stepping into the fullness of who I am capable of becoming?
- How must I change?

Take some deep breaths as you release all the ways in which you have been playing small so that you emerge into the majestic being you came here to be, on and off the golf course.

Take a couple of deep breaths as you allow this vision to sink in. (Allow yourself a few moments to integrate the new information.)

And now with this next breath, open yourself to the next questions:

- What must I embrace?
- How can I step into the feeling vibration of this vision?
- What can I do to activate this quality within me?
- What new habits must I establish to create the emotional and psychological and physical musculature around this vision?

Breathe deeply as you contemplate releasing all the layers that cover up the masterpiece that you are. (Allow yourself a few moments to integrate the new information.)

And now with this next breath, open yourself to the last questions:

- What specific action steps must I take?
- Is there something I can physically do as a representation of my inner commitment to become this vision that I see?
- Is there an action I can take? A person I can call? An exercise I can try? A clinic I can attend? Is there something I can do that will put me in alignment with the high vision of the golfer I am capable of becoming?

If it is clear to you what action to take, then make sure to write it down. And if the answers are not clear, then simply allow them to come to you in their time.

Take a couple of deep breaths as you allow this vision, these action steps, to sink in. (Allow yourself a few moments to integrate and write down the new information.)

In a few moments, you will begin to make your way back. You will begin to count upward from zero to five. Zero represents deep asleep, and five represents wide awake, completely awake and aware.

Starting with zero, deep asleep—go deeper than before. As you rest here in this deeply relaxing state, contemplate the following mantra:

"Each and every day, in every possible way, I am making progress. I am getting better as I am moving in the direction of my vision of the golfer I know I truly am. I am inspired and I am enjoying the process."

One—notice that you may be feeling physically relaxed and rejuvenated.

Two—recognize emotional calm expanding around you, reminding you that you are in the right place at the right time, doing the right thing.

Three—climb higher toward awakening as you become aware of the air on your skin. Slightly move your fingers and toes to signal that you are about to awaken, as you record all that you have just experienced deep in your subconscious mind.

Four—take a big deep breath and feel a tingling sensation, knowledge that your vision is becoming realized now simply because you shined the light of your awareness on it.

Five—now move up to five. With your eyes open, you are wide awake. You are now completely awake and aware, feeling wonderful.

Zone Golf Goal Setting

The difference between an amateur and a pro is that an amateur tries to hit the house, and a pro tries to hit the keyhole.

—*Greg Norman*

Now that you have done the Zone Golf visioning process and are in sync with the highest version of what it is you want from this program, it is time to begin the process of bringing that vision down to earth. Goal setting, when it is in alignment with your highest vision, is the most powerful step you can take toward becoming the best golfer you are capable of being.

While Zone Golf visioning took you out of your limited mind and connected you with (perhaps) a higher vision than you may have had before, Zone Golf goal setting will allow you to become clear about what it is that you need to do to actualize that vision—shot by shot, moment by moment. Zone Golf goal setting will assist you in placing your golf goals into your future so that they will actually occur. If you invest your attention on your intention, the highest ROI will be reflected in your low scores.

The Zone Golf goal-setting process is distinct from traditional goal setting in that it involves using self-hypnosis to help you take charge of your subconscious expectations of your golf game. When you take charge of your subconscious expectations of your golf game, you will produce results—you will be unable not to. Remember, when you deal with the subconscious mind, you are dealing with the 88 percent of your mind's power that runs the show of your life.

What very few people realize is that in life we don't get what we want, we get what we expect. And the problem is that most people go through life with unconscious expectations of failure. It has been said that having no expectations are expectations of "no." Most people show up on the golf course with unconscious expectations of failure. What you need to learn to do is take charge of your unconscious expectations as you navigate your golf game. Learning to do this gives you a level of mastery that will have beneficial results for your golf game and will make you extremely powerful in all aspects of your life, elevating you from victim to victor in a very short period of time.

The Zone Golf Goal-Setting Formula

Why do you want to go to the trouble of improving your game?

When you discover a powerful enough "why" that truly inspires you into action to become the best golfer you can be, you will bolt out of bed every day chomping at the bit to get to the golf course.

How will you feel, think, and act once you've discovered the "why" that springs you into action?

How would you feel if you were able to experience the level of mastery that enables you to materialize your goals before your eyes?

The Zone Golf goal-setting formula should be used whenever you have a golf goal that you really want to manifest. Even the word *Zone* is mnemonic to help you remember the process of Zone Golf goal setting.

ZONE Stands For

Zero in on the bull's-eye of the goal that you want to achieve.

Own the course, and open wide to see the big picture.

Now! Write your goal in positive, present-tense language as if it were happening right now. Navigate your way toward your goal.

Express your best self. Exaggerate the multisensory details of your goal to create a deeper emotional imprint in your subconscious mind.

Let's break it down into more detail.

Z: Zero In

What is the bull's-eye of your target? Include a date by which you would like this goal to be fulfilled.

For example, if you are a 19 handicap, you might set a goal of becoming a 9 handicap by the end of the season (a very lofty goal but a possible one).

On a yellow legal pad or in a journal, give yourself permission to write about the goal in as much detail as you would like and add in as many nuances as possible. If you have more than one golf goal, then repeat the process for each goal. Flesh out exactly what you want.

Think of this as a movie, and you are the director, star, and writer of your movie. So write the script to inspire you to want to watch your movie.

As you are writing your goal, consider the following five questions:

1. What do I want? (A 9 handicap.)
2. Why do I want it? (I will be living up to my potential, and I will know in a tangible way that I am improving. I will be able to be more competitive and have the confidence to compete in more tournaments. I will feel proud of myself.)
3. How will I get it? (I will practice the 28-day Zone Golf Program. I will book lessons with a pro once a week for the remainder of the season. I will focus every other lesson on improving my putting skills.)
4. When will I get it? (By October 31.)
5. How will I know when I reach my goal? (By accurately entering my golf scores in the register after each game, I will receive my official monthly handicap update from my local golf course at the end of

the season. I will open up this letter and see in black and white that my new handicap is 9!)

I firmly believe that an angel, not the devil, resides in the details. In my fifteen years of experience as a hypnotherapist, I've come to notice that when a person is brave enough to acknowledge and thus breathe life into the tiniest nuances of their desires, that is when commitment takes place, and that is when the magic kicks in.

I find that most people avoid the details about what they most deeply desire because it puts them into a far more vulnerable position than they are comfortable being in. You could say that when people get down to the nitty-gritty of what it is they truly want, it is like they are wearing their heart on their sleeve.

Ultimately, if you are willing to live a life of passion and true fulfillment, it requires risk, losing one's cool, and looking like a fool (in the realm of the ego) if your goal does not unfold like you thought it should. The Zone Golf goal-setting process is not for the faint of heart. It is a hero's journey to be engaged in the action required to fulfill what it is that you truly want in life. Given the choice, the average person will be vague and unclear about what he or she wants.

The moment you zero in and become specific about the minute, microscopic essence of what it is exactly that you want, the entire universe shifts to support you. That is why I suggest that you tack on as a caveat to the end of each goal a quote from Shakti Gawain: "This or something better; for the highest good of all concerned."

With this caveat, you remain committed but detached, allowing just enough space in your airtight plan for grace to take place and for unseen advantages to come in and work on your behalf. So if your goal doesn't occur exactly as you see it, instead of being disappointed, know that this or something better must be occurring for the highest good of all concerned.

Once you've written down your goal with as much detail as you can muster, give it a headline. A headline is a single statement that encapsulates your goal with bullion-cube conciseness. For instance, "I, Kelly, consistently average two putts per hole."

Zeroing in on your goal and writing it down as a headline delivers it to your subconscious mind like an arrow moving with laser swiftness toward the bull's-eye of a target. Now your subconscious mind can wrap all of its resources (88 percent of your mind's power) around that goal to make it happen.

O: Own the Course

Act as if you were the king or queen of the green, like you own the place. It is your party and all the elements that make up the golf course and the game are here for you.

If I could wave a magic wand and give you a gift that would expedite your transformation as a golfer, it would be *confidence*. Because golf is about managing mistakes, rarely do even the best golfers execute their shot exactly as they see it, and there is a natural humility built into the game. People can never get too cocky or sure of themselves in this game. For this reason, all golfers whom I know and work with benefit from a strong injection of confidence. Act as if you own the place. Of course,

I'm not suggesting that you speak this aloud and become obnoxious about it, but act as if the course were entirely yours, that you have the right to be there regardless of your skill level.

When you are teeing off or are standing on the putting green and remember that you own the place, yips disappear and your natural genius can emerge to the surface, regardless of the mistakes you make. When you own the place, you expect to make mistakes because that is part of the process. In fact, you know that the more mistakes you make, the better, because that means that you are actually on the fast track, taking risks toward becoming the best golfer you can be. When you own the place, you are out of your own way and can really play.

O also stands for open wide to see the big picture. If you could open your senses and open your mind wide to see and sense yourself as big and as great as you possibly could be, what would you see, feel, and sense?

Many people short-change their lifetime achievement potential by basing their worth on short-term high expectations. To open up to grasp the vastness of who you truly are and what you are capable of, it might help to see yourself from a third-party's perspective, perhaps from the vantage point of one who admires you or even from the perspective of your creator. As you journey into Zone Golf goal setting, dare to open, open, open, beyond what you think you are capable of, to the grand vision of your best self.

Remember Mark Twain's famous novel *The Prince and the Pauper*? This archetypal story tells of two boys, very similar in appearance, one born of royalty and the other born into poverty. They switch roles and discover not only stark class inequalities but also the fact that they are both, essentially, noble. This story has been reproduced in numerous forms and has stood the test of time because it resonates with the heart of humanity. It is everyone's story. Consider that you are royalty in disguise, born for greatness, capable of more than you could ever realize. Remain *open* to the big picture of who you are as you are setting your goals so that you do not undercut yourself or sell yourself short.

Here is a disclaimer for the *o* in *Zone*. If you are one of those rare individuals who naturally dreams big, big, big, but never seems to manifest your desired outcome, then consider scaling your goal back a bit to make it more realistic, practical, and achievable.

The key is to aim high while remaining grounded to set up a record of success. Remember, there is nothing that breeds success like success, but you want to stretch yourself, to open to something larger, greater, better than you think you are capable of achieving.

Another way of looking at the *o* in *Zone* is from the perspective of oneness, whereby you reconnect with your sense of being intrinsically connected to the whole of life. Remind yourself that there is only one activity happening on the golf course, and that all things are inseparably woven into a single tapestry. See Secret #4 to learn more about this. The source of all stress emanates from a sense of separation from the whole, whereas the source of all well-being emanates from a sense of being connected to the whole.

When you think and say the word *oneness* silently to yourself as you approach the ball, you are putting yourself vibrationally in league with all the different systems that connect you with the ball, the hole, and your goal.

N: Now!

Write your goal in positive, present-tense language as if it were happening right now.

Another reason most people don't have success with a typical goal-setting process is that they write their goals in the future tense. Writing goals or thinking about goals in the future keeps them grasping at something that is always just out of arm's reach.

Write and create your goals in the present tense as if they were happening *now*, not next week or next month. Putting your golf goal in the present tense helps you build your "act as if" muscles, which place your present-tense reality in league with your future desires. As you do this there is an emotional, psychological elevation and synergy that takes place. When you collapse the future into the present, you powerfully rearrange your relationship to your goal and to the achievement of that which you truly desire.

If there is something that you desire and it is not coming to you, it always means the same thing. You are not a vibrational match to your own desire. Take the time to line up the Energy first, and action becomes inconsequential. If you don't take the time to line up the Energy, if you don't find the feeling place of what you're looking for, not enough action in the world will make any difference. Genius. It is just attention to something specific.
—Abraham-Hicks, © by Jerry & Esther Hicks

Albert Einstein said that time—past, present, future—occurs simultaneously, and it is an illusion of consciousness that these aspects of time operate independently of one another. When you can picture your future goal but speak as if it were happening now, then you quicken the process of aligning who you are now with who you will have to be to fulfill that goal.

For example, if you desire to win a tournament, say, "I, [your name], am so thrilled that I won the PGA Championship and am holding the Wanamaker Trophy in my hand."

Nothing will change until you say, "Right here, right now, my success is now. Right now I am the best golfer I can be, right now." Feel the feelings of this success from the ends of your fingers to the tips of your toes.

As you are affirming your goals in the present tense, you want to also keep them positive (or think of *n* as also standing for "not negative"). This is another piece of the puzzle that causes Zone Golf goal setting to create results. There are so many people who state their goals in a negative way. For example,

"I hope I don't blow this game."

"I hope I don't get the yips again on this putt."

"I hope I don't embarrass myself as badly as I did last time."

You can reframe your thought to change self-criticism into opportunities to learn. For example,

"Even though I missed that shot, I now know how I will handle it better the next time."

"I am getting better every day and learning as I go."

"I am proud of the progress I am making, knowing that I am learning from my mistakes and making constant improvements."

You can't think about what you don't want to think about without thinking about it. Think about that!
—Christopher Howard, International leader
in neurolinguistic programming

The unconscious mind does not process negatives directly. So if I say to you, don't think of Tiger Woods, what do you think of?

Even if you say, "I didn't think of Tiger Woods. I thought of Annika Sorenstam," it was still an *indirect* process. You had to think of Tiger Woods and then switch channels as you pulled up the image of Annika Sorenstam.

Placing your goals into a positive framework and wording them affirmatively is about directionalizing your focus in a way that allows you to produce extraordinary results. For example,

"I, [your name], just completed a _____ game with ____ under/over par, my best game ever, and I feel wonderful."

Now, when you write your Zone Golf goal in a positive and present way, you want to state it exactly as you would like it to happen.

N can also stand for "navigate." Navigate the particular way you will fulfill your goal. Visually see a line drawn in the grass from your ball to the hole. Navigate the direction in which you have to hit the ball to compensate for the hills, bumps, wind, and any obstacles blocking your path.

Navigate the way in which you will implement all that you've learned in your golf lessons, suggestions from the pros, the finger position on the club, your posture, the placement of your elbows, and your practice swings.

E: Express Your Best Self

Enthusiasm is one of the most powerful engines of success. When you do a thing, do it with all your might. Put your whole soul into it. Stamp it with your own personality. Be active, energetic and faithful, and you will accomplish your object. Nothing great was ever achieved without enthusiasm.
—*Ralph Waldo Emerson*

Let it rip. Now that you've aligned your body, mind, and spirit with your goal, exhale and express yourself. This is the part of the formula in which you take all that you've been intending, all that you've been preparing for, and simply let go and have fun.

Stop waiting to exhale. Take a deep breath and release the tension of your day—all your planning, struggling, manipulating, managing—and simply let go.

Imagine that when it comes to actually making contact, club to ball, tension is the enemy of your successful golf game. Inspiration cannot come into a tense environment.

While you're at it, enjoy yourself—enjoy the game, enjoy the freedom that allows you the opportunity to play this game, enjoy the wind on your face, the sun warming your body, the smell of freshly cut grass and flowers.

E also stands for "exaggerate." Create a deeper emotional imprint in your subconscious mind of the goal you are working toward by exaggerating the image in your mind's eye. This is where your "imagic-nation" comes in.

Imagination is more important than knowledge. For knowledge is limited, whereas imagination embraces the entire world, stimulating progress, giving birth to evolution.

—*Albert Einstein*

For example, if your goal is to be able to tee off long and straight, then you might picture yourself standing in a larger-than-life scenario, ten feet tall, and your golf club the size of a pencil, and then simply imagine drawing a line with the pencil directly to where you want the ball to land. Or imagine that there is a magnetic strip right beneath the grass lining up directly from the tee to the green, and when you tee off, you see and feel the straight shot sailing powerfully across the course, undeniably to the exact spot where you intend it to land.

The reason for exaggerating your sensory perception of your goal is to lodge your goal as deeply as possible in your subconscious mind as quickly as possible. So when you set a goal, you want to engineer it to shock you in a positive and extraordinary way for it to influence your subconscious mind to operate automatically. Imagine being able to step out on the golf course, automatically feeling confident, hitting the ball long and straight, and being able to putt with confidence and control, without even having to think about it.

The only limit to your impact is your imagination and commitment.
—Anthony Robbins , peak performance coach and author of
Awaken the Giant Within

Once you've written down your goal, you want your imagination to see or feel yourself identifying that final puzzle piece that will make it happen. When that happens, you know you've got the goal (is it your improved scorecard or a picture in the paper for achieving your goal or a trophy in your hand—what does the physical evidence of your success look like?).

Time Stream

Sir Isaac Newton described time as like a railroad track that stretched infinitely in two directions. Later, Einstein's theory of relativity expanded on all previous concepts of time to say that you can't separate time from space. Einstein said that time was relative to the observer and that each individual has his or her own unique interpretation of time. And each of us, therefore, has our own "time stream."

The hypnotherapist Tad James says that the time stream is simply the way you imagine time to flow. Some people say that it seems like the past is behind them and the future is in front of them. Some envision their past as being to their left or to their right and their future in the opposite direction. Take a moment to consider where you envision your past and your future.

There is no right way or wrong way—how each individual imagines it is different. The point is for you to visualize where the future takes place for you so that you can take your Zone Golf goal and place it into your future time stream, where it will actually occur.

Preparing for the Zone Golf Goal-Setting Self-Hypnosis Script

Because the Zone Golf Goal Setting self-hypnosis script is one of the most powerful scripts in this program, it requires a bit of preparation. The following is a list that reiterates all that you need to do before your self-hypnosis session so that you can prepare yourself for a truly transformational experience.

Before starting the script,

1. Zero in on the bull's-eye of the goal that you want to achieve.
   Write this down so that it is clear, by answering the following questions:

   • What do I want?
   • Why do I want it?
   • How will I get it?
   • When will I get it?
   • How will I know when I reach my goal?

Close your eyes and relax. Use your imagination (imagic-nation) to step inside the goal you have written in such a way that you feel that you are actually inside of it. Look at all the details of your goal in Technicolor. Hear the sounds around you and feel the sensations of being viscerally inside your golf goal.

2. Imagine that you own the course, as you open wide to see the big picture. Imagine that you are the king or queen of the golf course. It is your party and all the elements that make up the golf course and the game are here for you. Allow yourself to connect with a feeling of oneness, to the whole of life, at one with the fulfillment of your goal, vibrationally in league with all the different systems that connect you with the ball, the hole, and your goal.

3. Now! Imagine that you are stepping inside your goal, as if it were happening right now. Then you will navigate the particular ways in which you will fulfill your goal. Visually see a line drawn in the grass from your ball to the hole. Navigate the direction in which you will have to hit the ball to compensate for the hills, bumps, wind, your finger position on the club, your posture, the placement of your elbows, and your slow-motion swing.

And as you are right there inside of your golf goal, adjust the qualities of the picture, the quality and volume of the sounds around you. You also may become aware of the feelings that are present, the level of their intensity, and the physical location in your body in which you notice the sensation. Maybe you will choose to turn up the intensity of the feeling. Work with all the qualities to make it the most full-bodied, multisensory experience for you.

4. Express yourself. See yourself playing with all your might, exaggerating the qualities as you breathe and exhale. You also want to make sure that once you've written down your goal, your imagination sees or feels yourself identifying a piece of evidence that proves that you have achieved your goal. For example, have you played three games in a row with the score you want? Are you no longer afraid? Are you standing on the green looking up with your club in the air, feeling the cool morning air on your skin, smiling excitedly because you just beat your best score?

And now, using the Zone Golf goal-setting formula, write your golf goal. For example,

"It is now [a date in the future]. I, [your name], am/have [evidence of having achieved your goal]."

Fill in the formula with your own information. For example, it might look like this:

"It is now August 8, 2012. I, Kelly Sullivan Walden, am standing on the golf course in Pebble Beach. I look over the course and realize that I now have a 9 handicap."

Make sure, when you write it down, that you include clear evidence that illustrates how you know you have achieved your goal.

Once you've written down your goal and imagined it in the most compelling, colorful, real, and exciting way possible, step back out of it but leave your body in the picture.

That is the goal-setting process.

Zone Golf Goal-Setting Self-Hypnosis Script

To prepare yourself, I suggest that you read your goal prior to diving in to this script so that it is fresh in your mind.

Your Zone Golf Hypnosis Journey

Sit in a comfortable, quiet position, or recline with your head slightly elevated.

Uncross your arms and legs, and rest your hands, palms up, either by your sides or on your thighs.

Should an emergency arise at any time while in self-hypnosis, you can get up to take care of the situation simply by counting yourself up from zero to five. At five you will be wide awake, completely alert, and aware.

Close your eyes and nod your head slightly, signaling to your subconscious mind that you are ready to enter a deep state of self-hypnosis to radically improve your golf game.

As you begin, take a few very deep breaths, and you may begin to notice certain parts of your body relaxing. Perhaps other parts are still a little tense. Just become aware of this, as your body continues to relax—the way your clothes feel on your body, the way the air feels as it gently brushes up against your face.

Notice your body being completely supported by the weight of the chair, couch, bed, or whatever it is that is holding you up.

As you read this, become aware of how good it feels to breathe in deeply and slowly, and to release completely. Feel your chest and stomach rise with each inhalation, and contract with each exhalation. Notice the release and the letting go that takes place now. With each breath that you exhale, you release all your cares of the day.

With each breath you breathe out, you let go of any and all tension that may linger in your body. And with each and every inhalation, you breathe in a sense of peace and relaxation.

Begin to count yourself down into a deeper state of relaxation. Start with five and move down to zero. At zero you will go deep asleep, a receptive state of focused relaxation. And with each count, you become more and more relaxed, and completely peaceful.

Begin with five, as you let go with each breath.

Four—all tension washes away.

Three—allow yourself to feel heavy in the chair or on whatever surface holds you up.

Two—let go more than before, as you prepare yourself to discover an inner resourcefulness that will improve the way you approach your golf game and relate to yourself as a golfer.

One—prepare to enter the Zone.

Zero—deep asleep. Each and every time you read or hear "deep asleep," you go quickly, soundly, and deeply to this depth or deeper for the purpose of entering the Zone and radically transforming your mental golf game.

You are hearing the sounds around you and feeling the feelings of being right there inside the goal. Get a sense of the date by which you said the goal would take place, and step right inside your goal. Imagine now that you are inside the goal, looking at it, right now.

And as you are inside that goal, notice your inner dialogue. What words do you say to yourself when you think of having made this golf goal happen now?

Become aware of the tone and resonance of your inner dialogue.

You are becoming comfortable inside this goal, and now it is time to adjust some of the qualities of the picture. These are like the buttons on your television's remote control. You are adjusting the scene to make it the most inspirational for you. Notice any sounds around you that stand out. If you need to change the volume of these sounds, then make that adjustment by turning them up or down.

You have the ability to add movement to this picture, like the wind blowing or your body moving in perfect grace.

You can enhance the color and brightness to make it the most appealing scene possible for you. If you need to adjust the speed of the movement, you can speed the scene up or put it in slow motion. Find what feels most pleasing to you.

Now notice the feeling tone in your body. Notice whether there is a specific location of the sensation, intensity, or vibration. Give yourself permission to take your remote control and amplify the feeling as much as you can with your next breaths. As you do this, you are anchoring this feeling deep in your subconscious mind. Take two more deep breaths as you double this wonderful sensation that you are present to, right now.

Now imagine that someone has taken a Polaroid picture of you in this victorious moment of fulfilling your goal. Once you are handed the snapshot, you can step out of that moment in time while leaving your body in the picture. See yourself in the picture that portrays you attaining that goal.

Now it is time to take that picture in your hands and in your mind's eye and go ahead and rise all the way up in the air. Take a few deep breaths, elevating higher and higher, all the way up above the time stream. Once you've risen to such a high vantage point, you can look down on everything now. From way up here, you might notice the past in one direction and the future in another direction. From way up here, even your glorious visions and golf goals seem small, even trivial, because you are connected to such a greater sense of yourself.

Now it is time to breathe your commitment into this photo. As you take three deep breaths and exhale them into the picture, you activate the photo and all that it represents with your intent. Go ahead and inhale and exhale three times as you commit to manifesting that picture.

Very good. Now that you have done this, everything you need to achieve your goal is beginning to line up.

Take a few moments to allow yourself to simply float here, appreciating the levity of being connected to this vast, expansive energy. And now, at the speed of thought, beam yourself into the future—place yourself right over that date in the future when you said your golf goal would occur.

When you are ready, release your snapshot into the time stream. See and feel the photo that has been energized with your intent drop all the way down to the day and time in the future when you said your golf goal would occur. Take a deep breath as you let it all go, starting right now.

You can now let this goal go because you realize that the universe is responding to your intent. With this powerful intent, you not only have influenced your future but also can look into the direction that represents your past and see that it has changed to support this new reality you have set forth. Now look way off into the distant future, and see that a new series of events is going to occur as a ripple effect of the reality you set in motion. (Allow a few moments of silence to contemplate this.)

As you become immersed in your future as a result of seeing your successful goal, notice everything becoming brighter, more brilliant, and more alive. Your goal has not just affected your time stream; it has influenced the streams of all those with whom you interact, throughout time and for generations to come.

Use these next few breaths to absorb all that you have just experienced. (Allow a few moments of silence to contemplate this.)

Now allow yourself, as you count upward from zero to five, to slowly, gently bring yourself back into the present moment, into the room where you are, into the now.

Zero—going deep asleep, quickly, soundly, deeply to this depth or deeper.

One—gently feel your physical body tingle and begin to awaken.

Two—you are now feeling emotionally calm, rested, and expanded, integrating all that you experienced deep into your cells and into the marrow of your bones.

Three—Notice a feeling of well-being flooding your entire being.

Four—feel a sensation of gratitude welling up in you for yourself, for your willingness to dare to dream, to set a goal, and to imagine it fulfilled. Know that changes have already begun in your golf game and in your life.

Five—with excitement, allow your eyes to open as you become wide awake, alert, and aware, and feeling great!

Secret Takeaways

- First create your desired outcome in your mind, then put your body to work to bring the goal into a realized state.
- The way we do any one thing will show us how we approach our entire life.
- We don't get what we want; we get what we expect.
- No expectations are expectations of "no."
- Many people short change their lifetime achievement potential by basing their worth on short-term high-expectations and underestimating their long term possibilities.
- Celebrate the micro-milestones—don't be a miser with your pat-yourself-on-the-back ability.

LOSE YOUR MIND AND WIN THE GAME

Turn your thinking on its head and become the master of your mind

One of the things that my parents have taught me is never listen to other people's expectations. You should live your own life and live up to your own expectations, and those are the only things I really care about it.

—*Tiger Woods*

Secret Synopsis

When you master your mind, you discover your ability to neutralize your inner critic while turning up the volume of your inner champion.

Get Out of Your Head and Into the Zone

Have you ever been in the Zone—even for only one shot?

When you were in the Zone, you experienced the perfect swing and you were playing to your true potential. Even if you haven't yet experienced it in your golf game, no doubt you've experienced a moment when you were out of your mind and completely in your body, in the moment. If you've done it once, then you can repeat it, because the Zone is already encoded into your mind and in your cells. You could say that being in the Zone is actually your nature, and that it is against your nature not to be in the Zone.

According to the Hypnosis Motivation Institute and the American Hypnosis Association, we only use 12 percent of our mind's power, leaving 88 percent, which is our subconscious mind, untapped. As the Zone becomes more of a habitual way of being, you will inadvertently access that mysterious 88 percent to "quicken" your way not only to improving your golf game but also to becoming a more actualized human being.

A relaxed state of being is half the battle of getting into the Zone. Tightening up and trying to steer the ball causes golfers to miss shot after shot. Being relaxed, being loose, and feeling confident will help you to play great golf. By practicing the self-hypnosis techniques outlined in this chapter, you will quickly and easily begin to feel relaxed, confident, and in the Zone.

Consider the reality that great golfers are simply ordinary people who know how to take the journey from their mind into the body, on command, and allow the body to do what it has been trained to do. You are no different from these individuals. You, too, are capable of making great shots. You, too, are capable of performing at a level that you can be proud of, and hypnosis is one of the most direct routes to get you there.

When you program your subconscious mind before you play with positive messages about your ability to improve your golf game, you will be in a much better position than if you were thinking your way through every shot.

A brief exercise can show us quickly how the body gets in the way of the mind:

Step 1: Get a pen and a piece of paper.

Step 2: Write your signature.

Step 3: Trace back over your signature.

Notice how awkward it was to trace your own signature? When you first wrote your signature, you weren't thinking about it. Your body took over, and it was effortless and perfect. When you traced back over your signature and went outside the lines, it was because you were thinking about it.

Michelangelo's *David*

It has been said that when Michelangelo was asked how he created the statue of David, he replied simply that David already existed beneath the marble, and all the artist had to do was to set him free by chipping away the excess marble.

This is exactly the process of "losing your mind" to win at the game of golf. This program, more than adding anything to you, assists you in releasing the excess marble that obscures the genius golfer you truly are.

With this book and accompanying self-hypnosis sessions, you will become more empowered, peaceful, confident, and successful as you improve your golf game. You will see a difference in how you feel, and you will enjoy your golf game today as you improve your swing, your putt, and your overall performance.

The Inner Critic: The Gargoyle at the Gate

If the Zone had a chief stumbling block, or a gargoyle at the gate whose job it was to keep you out of the Zone, it would be the inner critic. In my research and experience, I've found that the original purpose of gargoyles was for their hideousness to scare people into being vigilant or to deflect unwelcome energy from entering the cathedrals they were guarding. But the irony about a grotesque gargoyle is that it tends to create a self-fulfilling prophecy: the fear and negativity it is guarding against seems to be the very thing it attracts. Upon gazing at its distorted face, you become scared and thus conjure a feeling of negativity of which you may have been previously completely unaware. It is the same thing with the inner critic. For example, when you hear your inner critic screech at you, *"Don't screw up this shot!"* how do think your next shot is going to go?

If you are unfamiliar with the term *inner critic*, let me give you a few more examples of what the inner critic's voice sounds like:

"I can't believe you blew that shot; any hack could've sunk that!"

"You couldn't hit the green with a sledgehammer!"

"Just when you were ahead of the game, you had to go and blow that last putt. What a loser; you do this every time."

"Why is it that you can control just about everything else in your life, but you just can't seem to be able to get a handle on your stupid golf game?"

"That was the easiest putt in the whole world, and you screwed it up. I wish the hole was a little bigger, so you could bury your head in it!"

"It's a good thing you bought that expensive driver with the titanium shaft and the melon-sized sweet spot so you can slice the ball even further into the trees."

The inner critic speaks with such authority; it is as if the critic were the final word on your status as a golfer, and as a human being for that matter. Notice how the inner critic goes right for your jugular, how it kicks you when you are already down, how it mercilessly runs your already splintered self-worth into the ground at the most "critical" moment.

Your inner critic is as menacing and ferocious as any bully on the playground has ever been and is as masochistic as any demeaning authority figure who has taken pleasure in pulverizing your fragile self-worth.

Why is that? What have we ever done to deserve such torment? And what can we possibly do to avenge such a villain? Kill it? Get a lobotomy? Pretend it's not there? Use affirmations?

Haven't we tried all these ways (OK, maybe not the lobotomy) to no avail? The only way to successfully deal with the inner critic and thus find the entryway into the Zone is to stop resisting! You already know that what you resist persists!

Kill 'Em with Kindness

I have found that one successful way of dealing with the inner critic is to treat it the way you would if you had a nagging mother in town visiting you. You know that underneath all her pessimism and naysaying, she means well; that she is not innately evil; that she is really not out to hurt you and crush your self-worth.

If you were to ask this nagging mother why she is so negative, she would reply, "I'm only trying to look out for your best interest, darling. Somebody's gotta do it, so it might as well be me."

You cannot restore someone to their Connection with Source by belittling them or by punishing them, or by being disgusted with them. It is only through love that you can return anyone to love.
—Abraham-Hicks, © by Jerry & Esther Hicks

Kindness and tact are a luxury that protective parents think they cannot afford. According to parents, your life is in jeopardy. And if they don't scream at you to get out of the middle of the street, that semitruck that you don't see just might run you over! The inner critic represents the primitive part of our minds: the limbic region, to be more specific. This is the part of us carried over from the days of living in caves that was concerned about nothing more and nothing less than survival—not getting eaten by a saber-toothed tiger.

So, as with a nagging mother who has come to visit, give your inner critic a big hug and turn a deaf ear to everything your critic has to say. Imagine that when your critic speaks, you are watching a foreign film, so instead of even trying to make out what it is saying to you, you simply read the subtitles at the bottom of the screen that read, "I love you, I care about you, and I want to make sure that you survive; I love you, I care about you, and I want to make sure that you survive…"

Instead of punching your critic in the nose or buckling in defeat, give it a hug, nod your head, and keep reading the subtitles. If you do this, ultimately the inner critic will simply become white noise that you barely notice—taking up zero of your energy, concentration, or confidence.

Mind Mastery

Another way of saying "lose your mind" is perhaps the more affirmative "master your mind." The goal is to have a mind without your mind having you.

My dog, Woofie, is a gigantically fluffy husky-keeshond mix, obviously bred to be a sled puller. During my daily tug-of-war with her, affectionately known as Woofie walks, my neighbors chide, "Are you walking your dog or is she walking you?" Ha, ha—very funny, I say, as my arm is being dislocated.

I think of the mind in the same way: who is thinking who? When the mind runs away with you, dragging you through the mud of self-criticism, then clearly it is the mind that is master. The way to enter the Zone, however, is to turn your thinking on its head.

Because golf is a gentleman's and a gentlewoman's game, you do not have the luxury of physically outrunning your mind like athletes do in football, basketball, or hockey. Those competitors have an advantage that is summed up in the saying, "You can't hit a moving target." In golf, you are a sitting duck. Unlike your fellow compatriots in more macho sports, you are not running, throwing, or punching. Your mind is sitting still like a billboard with a neon "kick me" sign in the middle beckoning your inner critic to lash out.

If your desire is to truly become a better golfer and a master of the Zone, then (here's the punch line) the most important thing you have to realize is that you have no choice but to transform your mind into your greatest ally.

The following self-hypnosis script on mind mastery will assist you in navigating your way past the hurdles of your inner critic so that you can chart your way with more acuity to the Zone.

Preparing for the Mind-Mastery Self-Hypnosis Script

In this self-hypnosis script, you will learn to relax, and you will go into a deep state where your subconscious mind, the powerful 88 percent, will take care of you as it directs your inner transformation. As this happens, you will be given X-ray vision to see beyond the berating of the inner critic so that mind mastery can occur. When this happens, not only will your golf game improve but also the enjoyment and experience of all areas of your life will be enhanced.

Read or listen to this self-hypnosis script whenever you are feeling anxious or stressed, whenever you just want to relax, feel refreshed, rejuvenated, or energized. The ideal time to embark on this script is first thing in the morning before a golf game or in the evening the night before a game. These are times when your body and mind are most naturally suggestible and receptive to the positive information that can create long-lasting results.

You will discover after learning how to put yourself in this deep, relaxed, hypnotic state that each and every time you read or hear the words "deep asleep," you will effortlessly go into a state of deep and total relaxation for the purpose of improving your golf game.

Mind-Mastery Self-Hypnosis Script

Your Zone Golf Hypnosis Journey

Sit in a comfortable, quiet position, or recline with your head slightly elevated.

Uncross your arms and legs, and rest your hands, palms up, either by your sides or on your thighs.

Should an emergency arise at any time while in self-hypnosis, you can get up to take care of the situation simply by counting yourself up from zero to five. At five you will be wide awake, completely alert, and aware.

Close your eyes and nod your head slightly, signaling to your subconscious mind that you are ready to enter a deep state of self-hypnosis to radically improve your golf game.

As you begin, take a few very deep breaths, and you may begin to notice certain parts of your body relaxing. Perhaps other parts are still a little tense. Just become aware of this, as your body continues to relax—the way your clothes feel on your body, the way the air feels as it gently brushes up against your face.

Notice your body being completely supported by the weight of the chair, couch, bed, or whatever it is that is holding you up.

As you read this, become aware of how good it feels to breathe in deeply and slowly, and to release completely. Feel your chest and stomach rise with each inhalation, and contract with each exhalation. Notice the release and the letting go that takes place now. With each breath that you exhale, you release all your cares of the day.

With each breath you breathe out, you let go of any and all tension that may linger in your body. And with each and every inhalation, you breathe in a sense of peace and relaxation.

Begin to count yourself down into a deeper state of relaxation. Start with five and move down to zero. At zero you will go deep asleep, a receptive state of focused relaxation. And with each count, you become more and more relaxed, and completely peaceful.

Begin with five, as you let go with each breath.

Four—all tension washes away.

Three—allow yourself to feel heavy in the chair or on whatever surface holds you up.

Two—let go more than before, as you prepare yourself to discover an inner resourcefulness that will improve the way you approach your golf game and relate to yourself as a golfer.

One—prepare to enter the Zone.

Zero—deep asleep. Each and every time you read or hear "deep asleep," you go quickly, soundly, and deeply to this depth or deeper for the purpose of entering the Zone and radically transforming your mental golf game.

On your next deep inhalation, hold it for a count backward from eight to zero. Eight, seven, six, five, four, three, two, one. And release completely.

Now hold the next breath in for a count of six. Six, five, four, three, two, one. Now hold your breath for a count of four—four, three, two, one—and release completely. Resume breathing normally, drifting into a deeper and deeper state of relaxation, opening your mind to greater levels of mastery, allowing yourself to become the best golfer you can possibly be.

During this session, you will address your subconscious mind, that part of you that is responsible for transformation and growth. This part of your mind controls the buttons, switches, and levers of your mind's power. This part of you has X-ray vision to see through any mental fog from your conscious mind, through to the truth in every situation. Acknowledge your subconscious mind for all the ways it supports you throughout your day. Thank it for taking such good care of you all these years. Take a deep breath of gratitude for all the automatic functioning that is happening with you that doesn't require your deliberate control, for example, your breathing, your blood flow, your digestion, and the continuous beating of your heart.

And now ask your subconscious mind to work with you to align your mind and body in the perfect way to remove any tension or stress you might have taken in today, yesterday, or at any time. Allow for the growth and productivity, creativity, self-confidence, strength, discipline, focus, and power to come to you as you now enter the Zone.

Each and every time you read or hear the word *Zone*, you immediately feel a peacefulness wash over you, all stress dissolves, and you become open to behold a vision of yourself as your highest and greatest possibility.

Count backward from ten to zero. With each count, you will find yourself going deeper and deeper into relaxation—a state of wonderful floating, a deep trancelike state that is safe and secure, and in which you are always in control.

Give yourself full permission to indulge as completely as you like in the suggestions that can and will positively alter your golf game and your life.

As you continue breathing normally now, feel the warmth of a great, calming, warming, golden light, like the sun, surrounding you from above. This warm, loving light enters through the top of your head, as you begin counting.

Ten—the relaxation moves down through the crown of your head, opening up the skylight of your mind, allowing the sunlight to pour through, smoothing out any lines on your face, cleansing any worry away. The relaxation moves down through your eyes that are feeling so heavy now, as the muscles relax. You can try to open them, but it's so much easier to allow those totally relaxed muscles to just remain closed. The relaxation moves down further and further through your cheeks, jaw, and even your teeth.

Nine—this wonderful sensation makes its way down through your neck and shoulders, like a light tingling down through your arms, massaging your shoulders, releasing any tension whatsoever.

Eight—drifting down through your chest, as you take in another cleansing breath. This breath allows the relaxation to penetrate through your lungs and heart, which continues to beat without you needing to do a thing.

Seven—continue to feel the relaxation move down deeper and deeper into your stomach area, relaxing deep inside your back and stomach muscles.

Six—this sensation warms and relaxes you totally and completely. Like a sponge, you are soaking up the warmth and relaxation deep into your hips and pelvic area.

Five—relaxation is now flooding deeper down. With each exhalation you release a little more than you thought you could. This wonderful relaxation continues down through your thighs.

Four—imagine sunlight moving down through every atom, cell, and molecule of your being, as the sunlight moves deep down into your knees.

Three—the relaxation now moves down into your ankles.

Two—as it continues to move through your feet and through every single toe, you might notice your right foot beginning to tingle and then your left foot. Any last bit of tension blows out through the soles of your feet.

One—every ounce of your body is tingling with relaxation. Every cell is open, aware, and sparkling as your body prepares for deep and total relaxation.

Zero—deep asleep. Each and every time you read, hear, or think "deep asleep," you go quickly, soundly, and deeply to this depth or deeper, for the purpose of surrendering to a deeply receptive state of self-hypnosis to assist you in improving your golf game. Surrender now as you go deep asleep.

Turn the palm of your right hand face up. And imagine that placed in this hand is your inner critic. Take a few moments to imagine its voice, what it tells you, as best as you can. Listen to your inner critic without judgment, without restriction, without constriction, and without editing. If you need a nudge, imagine how you would feel if you were golfing with people you wanted to impress and you just shanked the ball into a bunker.

Go ahead and imagine your inner critic going to town on you. Notice what it says and the way it feels in your body. Imagine that this energy is now in the palm of your right hand.

If it had a color, what would it be? (Allow a few moments of silence between each question to contemplate your responses.)

What texture would it be?

What would it smell like, taste like?

If it had a name, what would it be?

If it could speak to you, what would it say?

Give your inner critic the space to say everything it wants to say to you about your golf game and about you as a golfer. What does it have to say about the game you will play next? Do not edit it.

Typically, we cut off our inner critic before it has gotten its rant out of its system. This tends to clog our system, and like a volcano, the inner critic has no choice but to blow at the most inopportune moments. However, by allowing it to blow off steam, just as you are doing right now, and by actually listening (something that rarely happens for the inner critic), you will notice its voice becoming calmer, more distant, less hostile.

Imagine now that you have on X-ray glasses that allow you to see through your inner critic. When you hear the voice of your inner critic speaking, picture the word *liar*. From now on, each and every time you feel the gripping panic of your inner critic, and there is no saber-toothed tiger leaping out from behind a tree, then you know it is simply an inappropriate fear response that is not relevant. Call a spade a spade—it is fear, it is a lie, and it is not something life threatening. See yourself smile, take a deep breath, and let it go.

Very good.

Continue to breathe all of this out as you focus your breathing into your stomach area, allowing all the muscles to release and let go around your abdomen, becoming completely relaxed.

Allow all negativity to wash away with each breath as you allow yourself to go deep asleep, quickly, soundly and deeply, to the depth you are at or deeper. Each and every time you hear or read "deep asleep," you go deep asleep for the purpose of self-improvement and becoming a better golfer. Deep asleep.

Now take another deep breath as you transition from the voice of the inner critic to the voice of your inner champion. Turn your left palm face up. Imagine your inner champion in the palm of your hand. Your inner champion is the part of you that is the most confident, the part of you that is wisest, smartest, brightest, clearest, most awake and aware. Take a couple of deep breaths as you contemplate this aspect of yourself. (Allow a few moments to take this in between each of the following questions.)

What color is your inner champion?

What texture is it?

What does it smell like?

What does it taste like?

If it had a name, what would it be?

Is there something it would like to say to you now?

Listen to what it has to say to you. Do not edit it. What does it have to say about the way you play golf?

What does it say about you as a golfer. As a person?

What advice does it have for you regarding the area in your game that is the most challenging for you?

What advice does it have for you about your next game?

Take a deep breath as you go deep asleep.

Continue to imagine your inner champion in your left hand, the color that it represents, and all of its qualities. Feel the pulse of your inner champion growing stronger and larger with each breath you take.

Simultaneously, imagine the inner critic in your right hand.

Feel the strength of your champion growing larger and larger. Imagine that it makes its way up your left arm, over your shoulder, and through your stomach, heart, and back. Feel the energy of your inner champion increase in intensity as it moves across your right shoulder and down your right arm, spiraling around and into your right hand. Your inner champion is growing stronger, larger, and more potent with each breath you take.

Slowly, with every beat of your heart, notice what begins to happen in your right hand. The colors from your inner critic and your inner champion begin to spiral and mix together, creating a new color, a new texture, a new smell and taste.

Notice the nuance of this new color, this new texture, this new smell and taste. This is the essence of who you are when you are no longer resisting your inner critic. This is the color that represents an integrated and evolved version of yourself merged with the largest of your highest self.

If this new, integrated energy had a name, what would it be?

Say this name silently to yourself three times and allow this name to be your new key word. This key word opens the door to the Zone for you, whenever and wherever you are, at your command.

What quality best describes this new energy?

What does this new voice have to say to you?

What advice does it have for you regarding your next game?

Once again, repeat silently your key word to yourself, and allow it to heighten and reactivate this feeling and higher awareness.

From this moment on, each and every time you say your new key word silently to yourself three times, it will be a trigger for you to enter this Zone of heightened awareness, peace, calm, and mental mastery.

Imagine yourself, now, on the golf course, about to tee off. You are standing, with your club gripped confidently in your hands. Each and every time your hands touch the club, you now associate this feeling with this key word, and you are automatically in the Zone of heightened awareness, peace, calm, and mental mastery.

Imagine now that every time you are about to hit the ball, whether it be to tee off, to putt, or to make a fairway shot, the grip of your hands on the club triggers the Zone of heightened awareness, peace, calm, and mental mastery.

Once more, say your key word to yourself three times. And each time you say it, you are flooded by the sensation of heightened awareness, peace, calm, and mental mastery—more intense than ever before. Imagine lining up your shot, taking in a deep breath, swinging the club, and making a solid connection with the ball. Watch it. A perfect shot, straight as an arrow. From now on, you will follow this pattern on each and every shot you make.

In these next few moments of silence, in your mind's eye, walk through your next game. See yourself taking a deep breath in and out, holding the club, and saying your key word three times silently to yourself, every time you grip the club. Each an every time you say this word, notice the sensation of the Zone becoming more clear, more visceral, more heightened, even more pleasurable. Mentally walk through the rest of your game now. (Allow a few minutes of silence.)

Now, imagine yourself in the clubhouse after your game, rewarding yourself with a nice, cool beverage. See that you have a smile on your face. In fact, you feel so good, that you can try as hard as you like not to smile, but you find that it is virtually impossible not to smile because you feel so good. Even now, the more you try to fight the smile, the more difficult it becomes because it feels so good to have mental mastery and to have just done such a great job playing a great round of golf in the Zone. As you drive home, you get a glimpse of yourself in your rearview mirror. As you do this, you notice that you are smiling because it feels so good to have your higher awareness, your inner champion, in the driver's seat giving you a new mental mastery and greater access to the Zone than ever before.

In a few moments, you will begin to count your way back from zero to five. Zero represents deep asleep, and five represents wide awake, completely awake and aware.

Zero—you go deep asleep, deeper than before.

One—begin moving your attention upward as you continue to feel physically relaxed, yet enlivened.

Two—as you are making your way up, you are feeling emotionally calm, peaceful, and happy, as if you were anticipating that something wonderful was about to happen to you.

Three—climb higher as you become aware of the air on your skin, and slightly move your fingers and toes to signal that you are about to awake. You are now integrating all that you have just experienced deep into your subconscious mind.

Four—you are waking up gradually as you take a big deep breath and feel a flood of well-being wash over you.

Five—move all the way up to awakening, as your eyes become open, wide awake. You are now completely awake, aware, and feeling great.

Secret Takeaways

- If you've been in the Zone at least once in your life, you can repeat it.
- Staying in a relaxed state of being is 88 percent of being in the Zone.

- Being in the Zone is when you, the club, the ball, and the range are one; when all the things that used to distract you seem miles away; and when you are focused, relaxed, and alert.
- Hypnosis is one of the most direct routes to get into the Zone.

Secret #3

THE HEART OF THE MATTER

Let your heart do the thinking

If my heart could do my thinking…[I would] know what's truly real.

—*Van Morrison*

("I Forgot That Love Existed")

> ### Secret Synopsis
>
> When your heart is chaotic, so are your mind and body, with the results being jerky swings and thoughtless misses. However, when you make a "you turn" from your head to your heart, you experience entrainment, giving rise to straight shots, dropped putts, and being more of the golfer you aspire to be.

The Zone is characterized by qualities of peace, tranquillity, ease, a slower pulse, a sense of focus, confidence, well-being, and a state of grace. Nowhere in that description is pensiveness.

Many golfers reflect wistfully on moments of having accidentally stumbled on the Zone in a golf game, like a time they witnessed a shooting star. Some think of the Zone as if it were as whimsical as a temperamental genie, appearing from a puff of smoke to help you out on that random day, for no apparent reason, just to get your hopes up. And then, like a cruel joke, as quickly as it appeared—poof!—it's gone, and you're back to triple bogeys!

Imagine for a moment that the Zone isn't elusive, isn't whimsical, isn't only for pros or for those with a genius IQ. What if the Zone isn't reserved only for the athlete-savants of the world or for those with golf obsessive-compulsive disorder? What if it is not a mysterious, mystical, illusive state at all? What if the Zone is actually closer to you than your breathing, more accessible to you than your American Express card, and more reliable than your Swiss watch?

You've heard me say things like that for several pages now, and if it hasn't yet caused you to throw the book across the room, then congratulate yourself for being one step closer to the Zone. Now, take a breath and consider for a moment that the Zone is actually a highly accessible state of consciousness that is possible to arrive at any time and everywhere. The trick is establishing the right habits and anchors that will make the Zone your default way of life, and in this chapter, we're going to focus on how to get there through the very center of your being.

Anchors Away

Creating anchors is one way to bypass the maze of the mind to get into the heart. Our lives are filled with anchors, from the simple (the morning sunrise symbolizing a new beginning) to the traumatic (the sight of an ambulance shooting shock waves through our nervous system) and the joyous (a bogey on a hole that you've always triple-bogeyed). Anchors are natural, automatic, and usually not something we consciously control. The goal, however, for the purposes of this program, is to bring them under your deliberate control.

A hypnotic anchor is an association you have between two things that are seemingly unrelated. For example, one of my personal anchors is the song "Back in the High Life" by Steve Winwood. When I hear this song, I am transported to the beach on the summer of my nineteenth birthday, smelling a barbecue, hearing the sounds of beach volleyball, feeling my sun-kissed skin and the salty air on my lips, and having an invincible feeling of "life is on my side" throughout my body. Hypnotic anchors use all our senses, sight, sound, smell, taste, and touch. When you intentionally create a hypnotic anchor, the more of your five senses you tie into it, the stronger and more powerful it becomes.

Ingredients of an Anchor

The following are ingredients of an anchor:

- Intent: Identify the state you want to achieve by creating the anchor.
- Personal relevance: Draw on your own experiences that have an impact on you.
- Sensory sensuality: The greater the number of senses (sight, sound, smell, taste, and touch) you can recall, the better.

The uses of anchors in golf are many. For example, let's say you're already in the Zone, in that hypnotic state of extreme well-being and heightened clarity and confidence, and you're on your favorite course. Once there, you contemplate the grass. As you do this repetitively, you will begin to associate the color green or even the sight of grass with feelings and thoughts that put you in the Zone.

Or you might associate a feeling of being in control by imagining a time in the past when you felt in control, that everything was going your way. If you do this several times while gripping your putter, you will begin to associate holding your golf clubs with having a grip on your game.

Create Your Personal Golf Anchors

To create your personal golf anchors, first, identify the hunger: what is your intended state of being (e.g., confidence, focus, energy, success) to accomplish the task at hand? What are you hungry for?

For example, if you know that you are prone to feeling tense or pressured at certain moments in your game, then a more conducive state of mind to make a particular shot or to achieve a desired outcome would be to be relaxed or at ease. Here are five steps to create your anchors:

1. What memory from your past (golf related or not) contains personal relevance and an imprint of this desired state of being? For example, you might recall a time when you were on vacation, swimming with the dolphins in the Bahamas, feeling completely relaxed, or a time when you received a raise or a promotion at work that was an acknowledgment of your prowess and ability.

2. Marinate in the feeling tone. Take three deep breaths as you luxuriate in the sensuality of this experience. Recall the sights, sounds, textures, tastes, scents, and feeling tone of that experience.

3. Magnify the sensations. As you practice this exercise, exaggerate your imagination of the desired feeling, including colors, sights, sounds, tastes, smells, and textures ten times stronger than you actually remember it. This will help to indelibly imprint this association in your mind.

4. Lock in on a nearby object. What do you see around you? If you are on the golf course, your eyes might lock in on freshly cut grass. Touch the grass or pluck a blade of grass and hold it in your left hand as you begin to associate this deeply relaxed feeling tone with your proximity to grass. If you are not on the golf course as you do this, imagine that you have a blade of grass, a tee, a club, or a golf ball in your right hand as you press your forefinger and thumb of your left hand together. Several times throughout the day, practice collapsing your intensified memory with a physical aspect that you typically see on the golf course (e.g., the relaxed feeling of swimming with dolphins associated with the green grass on the golf course).

5. Repetition, repetition, repetition. For the first week of the 28-day Zone Golf Program, you should practice these anchoring steps as much as possible. As you do this, you are creating a habitual groove in your subconscious mind, with the end result being that your anchor will happen automatically, without the need for your conscious control. For example, once your anchor is set in place, each

and every time you smell freshly cut grass, your mind will take you to a state of deep ease and control.

Keep in mind, human beings are habit makers, and if you can create the right kind of anchors with your habitual thoughts, you will become fluent in the Zone in your body and heart. As you do this, eventually everywhere you turn will be yet another anchor. You might try to go back to your old way of playing (on the outside of the Zone and looking in), but as hard as you try to go back, you will be unable to, because the Zone is your new way of being, naturally, habitually, and consistently.

You Turn

Point to yourself. Where on your body did you point to? I'd bet a million dollars that you did not point at your head but rather to your heart. Even though this way of identifying oneself, by pointing at the heart, is universal, most people, especially those in Western societies, associate themselves with their minds.

The trouble is, most minds are filled with criticism, especially the minds of golfers. We covered this in Secret #2, but because it is such an important and relevant topic, let's take it a step further. If you could reorient yourself to operate from your heart (literally and figuratively) and not your head, the Zone would be completely ordinary to you.

Your heart is the essential key in your ability to have an impact on your golf game and on your life. In Secret #2, you identified the inner critic for what it is, the voice of fear based on a caveman survival system that is no longer relevant. You will no longer be fooled into believing that just because the inner critic speaks with the authority of the Wizard of Oz that it is correct.

Now you have peeked behind the curtain and seen that the big, bad, voice of your inner critic is not the almighty Wizard of Oz but rather a shaky, flimsy, frightened, snively caricature with a bullhorn. You have blown its cover, and the jig is up.

Now what?

Now it is time to take a you turn.

Some say that the longest journey is the twelve inches from the head to the heart. But not for you. You've revealed the true identity of the inner critic, the gargoyle at the gate. Now there is nothing stopping you from entering the Zone. And the most direct route to the Zone is through your heart. According to Sheva Carr, a licensed teacher and practitioner of HeartMath (an institute that researches heart intelligence and stress management), the muscle of the heart is sixty times stronger than the brain, and its intelligence is far superior. It even has more power! As William Pawluk, MD, told SelfGrowth.com, "The heart muscle itself, because of its electrical activity, creates its own endogenous Electro Magnetic Frequencies (EMFs). Using a special magnetometer, one can see that the heart produces its own measurable, dynamic magnetic fields."

The heart has an eight-foot electromagnetic field beyond the circumference of your physical body, according to HeartMath, which is why if you have ever gone to the hospital for an electrocardiogram, the lab technicians are instructed to stand away from you during the test. If they stand too close, their hearts will influence your heart's reading. The force field of the brain can't do that—the brain doesn't have a force field.

Allowing yourself to take the time to become more heart centered as you approach your golf game will not only enhance your golf game but also have a positive effect on your relationships, your pocketbook, and many other aspects of your life as well.

Imagine a radio station that is full of static. Is that a radio station that you will stop to listen to? Of course not. It is difficult for your body and mind to get in sync with a heart that is frantic and staticky. However, when you can quiet your mind with the self-hypnosis scripts offered at the end of this chapter, then you will become a clear, clean transmitter of information. In other words, you will be a clear radio station—all the muscles, the joints, and the thousands of synapses that fire in sync—when your body, your mind, and your heart operate in synergy.

In essence, the goal of this chapter is to assist you in becoming the most synergistic heart-mind-body being you can possibly be so that you can have mastery over your inner state. When you have mastery over your inner state, you become immune to circumstance: foul weather, a missed shot, a wild shank—anything that might upset you and hook your attention away from being the clearest, laser-focused Zone golfer you can possibly be.

What we do and think repetitively creates a deeper and deeper groove in our subconscious mind and becomes automatic behavior. So if you pick and choose heart-centered habits that are on target with the results you want to attain, what would happen? Before you know it, you will finish 18 holes, look down at your scorecard, and see that you have just played the best game of your life. Everyone will ask, How did you do it? What's your secret? And you'll just smile confidently, shrug your shoulders modestly, and reply, "I guess I'm just in the Zone."

Let's get you there.

The Shortcut to the Zone—The Heart

In the following heart-centered Zone Golf self-hypnosis session, you will begin by focusing your attention with each breath on the area around your heart. With each breath, imagine that the area around your heart begins to soften, to loosen up, and that all barriers begin to dissolve. This is the true shortcut to the Zone.

You can practice this on and off the golf course. You do not need to be in a self-hypnosis session to access the enhanced state that this exercise provides. In fact, any time you feel yourself snagged by the inner critic (telltale signs: shortness of breath, increased pulse, negative thinking, and negative and edgy feelings), remember to take a you turn toward your heart and simply breathe in and out into your heart. Continue this heart-centered breathing exercise until you begin to notice your breath and your heartbeat becoming smooth and even, continue to hear and feel your heart beat beneath your chest and relax more and more with each and every breath.

Imagine that your heart is the orchestra conductor of your mind and body. When your heart is chaotic, so are your mind and your body, with the results being cacophony, missed shots, jerky swings, and thoughtless misses. However, when your heart beats in a peaceful, smooth rhythm, you are in an optimum state to experience a perfect swing. When you make a you turn and become more heart centered with your breathing, you create a context in which your mind and heart operate together in a harmonious, synergistic way, with the result being straight shots, dropped putts, and your being the golfer you dream of being.

Preparing for the Heart-Centered Zone Golf Self-Hypnosis Script: Your Hazard List

Golf is not a game of great shots. It's a game of the most accurate misses. The people who win make the smallest mistakes.

—*Gene Littler, professional golfer*

To prepare for this self-hypnosis exercise, write down a list of the most typical nagging reasons that you are upset on the golf course. In other words, make a list of the things that your inner critic is most apt to badger you about. Make that list now.

Your hazard list might look like this:

- Overflying the green
- Getting the yips on the green
- Slicing the ball off the fairway
- Knocking the ball into bunkers
- Double- or triple-bogeying

Keep that list nearby when you go into your self-hypnosis session. You will learn how to turn each of those thoughts inside out. When you are fixated only on what is wrong, you close off your ability to see the bigger picture. When you step back, and back further, you are able to access a wisdom that puts you in concert with all dimensions of your being and brings about harmony within you.

When you can look at each stressful thing in your life through the lens of your heart, then even irritating, challenging, difficult things become helpful to your growth. With practice, you will begin to discover the blessing in disguise in every situation. And you will learn in a very short time how to have a laser focus on the Zone.

As you transform the stress in your life on and off the golf course, you will become an agent of change simply because your heart-centeredness feeds into the electrical field of the entire planet. When you make the you turn from your head to your heart to the Zone, your impact ripples out from your improved golf game to your relation-ships and to the globe. From a unified field perspective, as one is lifted, all are lifted.

Heart-Centered Zone Golf Self-Hypnosis Script

Your Zone Golf Hypnosis Journey

Sit in a comfortable, quiet position, or recline with your head slightly elevated.

Uncross your arms and legs, and rest your hands, palms up, either by your sides or on your thighs.

Should an emergency arise at any time while in self-hypnosis, you can get up to take care of the situation simply by counting yourself up from zero to five. At five you will be wide awake, completely alert, and aware.

Close your eyes and nod your head slightly, signaling to your subconscious mind that you are ready to enter a deep state of self-hypnosis to radically improve your golf game. Take several deep breaths. As you breathe, imagine that you are breathing into your heart: inhaling into your heart and exhaling from your heart.

Focus your attention with each breath on the area around your heart. With each breath, imagine that the area around your heart begins to soften, to loosen up, and all barriers begin to dissolve.

Continue to focus your attention as you breathe into the area around your heart, until you begin to notice your heartbeat.

Notice it beginning to become a gentler rhythm than before, steady and coherent, smooth and even. Continue to hear and feel your heartbeat beneath your chest, and relax more and more with each and every breath you take.

As you continue this heart-centered breathing, count backward from five to zero. Allow each count to bring you deeper within your heart, starting with five.

Five—breathe into your heart.

Four—imagine that you are melting deeper to allow your body to synchronize with your heart.

Three—relax as you and your mind find their gentle connection with your heart and body.

Two—feel the synergy, the peacefulness.

One—enjoy this restful experience.

Zero—deep asleep.

Each and every time you think or read "deep asleep," you go quickly, soundly, and deeply to this depth or deeper, for the purposes of moving out of your head and into your heart. Deep asleep. You are now becoming deeply relaxed and peaceful.

Imagine that you are now on the golf course, playing very well because you are in sync with your heart, which is leading the way. Your mind is following the GPS system of your heart, which is directing the muscles and joints of your body to move in precision. Imagine this sensation, the way this looks, the way it sounds, the way it feels in your body, and the way it feels emotionally when all aspects of you are in sync.

Now, take a look at your hazard list and choose one of the items that has caused you stress and has stimulated your inner critic. Once you've identified the hazard, imagine it taking place and feel the corresponding stressful feelings that naturally occur.

Ground this by writing down the word that describes the way you feel when you have fallen into one of your hazards and your inner critic is raking you over the coals. Your word might be *panic, stress, despair, defeat, frustration, anger, blame, victimhood,* or even *annihilation, embarrassment, pain, anguish, worthlessness, rejection,* or *self-hatred.* Identify the word that most accurately describes the way you feel when your inner critic has taken over the show. (Allow a few moments of silence to contemplate this.)

Now, take a you turn and begin a heart-centered breathing exercise in which you simply come back to breathing in and out as you focus on the area around your heart. Continue to breathe in this way a few more times until you feel your heartbeat return to a softer rhythm.

Once you do this, try to identify your emotional state or the way you feel when your heart and mind have come back into peaceful connection. Write this word or words down. Some examples might be *peaceful*, *reassured*, *all is well*, *calm*, *wider perspective*, *grateful*, *worthy*, *successful*, *content*, *joyful*, and *well-being*. Take your time as you identify the word that most accurately describes the way you feel. (Allow a few moments of silence.)

Notice how quickly you are able to transition from feeling and thinking negatively about yourself to feeling good. Acknowledge yourself for demonstrating how quickly you are able to make a you turn. Take a deep breath and realize that you are well on your way to mastery.

Now let's try it again.

Once again, call an item off your hazard list to contemplate. Again, experience it in your mind's eye and observe the corresponding thought and feeling that the experience stimulates. Once again, write down the word that describes the hazardous experience.

Take a couple of deep breaths and take a you turn to begin your heart-centered breathing exercise, coming back to breathing in and out as you focus on the area around your heart. Continue a few more times until you feel your heartbeat return to a softer rhythm.

Once again, identify the word that describes your emotional state or the way you feel as your heart and mind are trained at last. Write the word down that most accurately describes the way you feel.

Again, notice how quickly, within minutes, maybe even moments, you were able to travel from your head to your heart and bypass the maze of the mind.

Now, as you continue to breathe into the area around your heart, amplify its wisdom by tapping into your heart's navigational GPS system, which has guidance it wants to share with you. Allow your heart to offer you an insight regarding the best course of action to take for each of the items on your hazard list. Take a few deep breaths as your heart informs you about how to best handle these situations.

Remain in the silence until you see, feel, or know what needs to be done, and you continue to breathe.

If it appears that you are not receiving any answers or if the guidance you receive does not make sense to you, don't worry. You are in the process of building a bridge from your conscious mind to your subconscious mind. If this process is brand new to you, be patient and give it time. Allow yourself the opportunity to be with whatever shows up in those seemingly empty moments and know that if you practice this process, soon you will begin to decode the invaluable messages that come to you from this practice.

Once you've received the insight to assist you in transforming your hazard list into fuel to empower you, give thanks to your heart for leading the way. Give thanks to your mind for being smart enough to sync up to the wisdom of the heart. And give thanks to your body for having such intelligence to operate so many functions automatically and effectively.

Know that as you count upward from zero to five, you can and will take this new tool with you onto the golf course to assist you in remaining in the Zone, improving your performance and keeping you feeling younger, healthier, and happier.

Zero—feel the strength and wisdom of your heart. Relax and connect with the feeling of synchronicity throughout your entire body.

One—begin to awaken. Notice your heart growing beyond the boundaries of your body, encompassing the entire golf course, the entire city you are in and beyond.

Two—move your awareness upward as you embrace the county, your state, and the world, bringing all of that power and intelligence back to your own heart within your body.

Three—you become more peaceful, more awake, more at ease, and excited about this mastery you have just learned and earned.

Four—take a deep breath.

Five—you are wide awake, completely awake and aware, and feeling wonderful.

Secret Takeaways

- Don't believe your own thoughts.
- Take a "you turn" to your heart.
- Your heart being coherent is the essential key in your ability to have an impact on your golf game, on your life, and on the world.

THE *ONE* IN *ZONE*

You are connected to everything and not separate from anything

Our separation from each other is an optical illusion of consciousness.
—Albert Einstein

We have only one problem of which there is only one solution. This singular problem is separation, and it has already been solved.
—Dr. Helen Schucman, from A Course in Miracles

Secret Synopsis

Einstein said that our separation is an optical illusion of consciousness. We perceive separation from the left hemisphere of our brain and unity from the right hemisphere. When you experience oneness on the golf course, you are accessing your right brain, which puts you in your "right" mind and releases your natural talent. This chapter will give you a quantum leap in your ability to enter into the Zone and stay there.

Connectivity

Quantum physics has revealed that the center of the universe is every-where and that its circumference is nowhere. From that perspective, the fact that you are alive and breathing means that you are connected with this center and thus connected to everything.

What does this mean for your golf game?

Imagine your hands taking their position on the golf club. It may look as if your hand and golf club are two separate things—but under a high-powered microscope you would see that there is actually a con-tinuum, a connecting fabric of atoms and electrons that maintains a web of unity between your hands and the club, the golf ball, the sky, the bunkers, the other golfers, the entire golf course. When you experience a state of connectivity to all that is on the golf course (and in all aspects of your life), you are truly in a power position, are at peace, and have greater access to the Zone.

Place your hands out in front of you, palms facing one another, as if you were holding a beach ball. Rotate your hands clockwise in small circles. Begin to notice a heat, friction, or tingling sensation between your hands. Now move your hand over an inanimate object (preferably a golf club or a golf ball) and you may notice a tingling, friction, or heat sensation—even though you are not touching the object!

If you and this object were truly separate from each other, then how could you communicate in this way? The reason is simple: you are not separate, and you are connected to everything. It is your perception of separation that feeds your illusion and keeps you at arm's length from the Zone. When you approach the golf course with the awareness of your connection to the unified field of all life, it will be nearly impossible for you not to maintain your access to the Zone.

Back in the Game

My father, an avid golfer, was diagnosed with spinal stenosis, a painful lower-back condition that causes severe sciatica. His lower disks had atrophied to such a degree that he was told to let go of his dreams of ever being able to golf again. And though he was devastated, he took the tragic news in stride. In spite of his optimism and bravado, it was clear that he was heartbroken. After five years of back and hip surgeries and two hip replacements, he is suddenly, by the grace of God, able to return to golf.

He called me after his first day out on his favorite course and reported with pride that his score was lower than it had ever been—after not golfing in five years! He said he truly appreciated every step, every shot, whether or not it went haywire. His appreciation, in this case, was the key to his well-being and gave him access to the Zone.

I attributed his amazing golf score to his lack of concern with his score and simply being grateful and connected to his fellow golfers while playing the game without the pressure that separation can create (e.g., "my game," "my score," "my shot"). In addition, during all the time he spent in the hospital and in recovery rooms, he was imagining in his mind's eye that he was out on the course, teeing off, swinging, hitting the shots as his best self. I'm sure that his visualizations contributed not only to the quantum leap in his golf score but also to his miraculous recovery.

Oneness

Oneness is pure consciousness, full and perfect. This manifest universe of matter, of names and forms being is full. This fullness has been projected from that fullness. When this fullness merges in that fullness, all that remains is fullness.

—*Isha Upanishad*

The self-hypnosis script in this section is dedicated to assisting you in accessing a state of oneness on and off the golf course—at will. Before you enter into this experience, let's explore a bit more about what the *one* in *Zone* really is.

Imagine two golf buddies who were once connected on their local golf course but now are separated and have relocated to different golf courses on different ends of the universe. They will remain connected and in communication, on some level, even though they are physically far apart. A web of connectivity unites objects and people—anything that is of this universe is inseparably connected, regardless of physical proximity.

It's a golf-related example of the butterfly effect, which says, in essence, that the flap of a butterfly's wings creates subtle changes in the atmosphere that may ultimately alter the wind in such a way as to accelerate, delay, or prevent a tornado from taking place on the other side of the planet. The flapping of the butterfly's wings is a small change that causes a chain reaction and results in large-scale alterations in events.

When you sneeze, someone on the other side of the world simultaneously says, "Bless you."

—*Rev. Michael Beckwith*

In quantum physics, Bell's theorem explores the mysterious and seemingly random ways in which separate places, things, and people affect and influence one another, even when they are separated by large distances. This theorem stimulates one to consider the profound relationship between the thoughts you think (golf related or not) and their effect on your golf game (and on your life itself).

In golf terms, this idea is exhibited by the way in which a subtle shift in your thoughts can have a drastic effect on your game, or by the way the wind will affect the direction a ball rolls into a bunker or right onto the green.

Separation without separateness is reality without rift.

—*Charles Williams*

If you think about Bell's theorem and the butterfly effect, you can begin to see that the physical world cannot be regarded as composed of distinct, separate entities. Even the most skeptical golfers can see that their thoughts (to some extent) set the tone for their experience on the golf course. For example, a client of mine says that when he golfs with a player who is slightly better than he is, his score always improves. His thoughts are hardwired in such a way that he genuinely believes that he will improve if he plays with someone who challenges him. Other golfers placed in the exact same situation, because of their core thoughts and beliefs, are affected in the exact opposite way.

It is done unto you as you believe.

—*Matthew 9:29*

Whether you think you can or you can't, either way you are right.

—*Henry Ford*

According to Gary Felder, PhD, Bell's theorem states that each part of the universe is a microcosm of the entire universe. From this perspective, you could say that the entire ocean resides within each drop of water; the entire sun exists within every sunbeam; and all the golfing genius of Tiger Woods, Arnold Palmer, and Annika Sorenstam resides, on some level, within you, right now.

When we realize that we are inseparably one with the whole of life, it is not such a stretch to recognize our connection with one another, with the animate and inanimate (our fellow golfers and our golf clubs), with that which we see (our scorecard) and that which resides on the furthest end of the galaxy.

We all have roots in the universe. Conscious mental activity exerts measurable effects on the physical world—a world that includes human bodies, organs, tissues, and cells... The inter-penetration of all matter is the rule... There is only one valid way, thus, to partake of the universe and that way is characterized by reverence—a reverence born of a felt sense of participation in the universe, of a kinship with all others and with all matter. A reverential attitude that bespeaks a oneness with the universe can transform the commonest act.

—*Bhagavad Gita*

Right Brain versus Left Brain

Traditional neurophysiology asserts that the left side of the brain is responsible for logical thought, speech, and reasoning, whereas the right side of the brain controls our feelings, emotions, and intuition.

It's your right brain that we want to focus on here. Your right brain connects you to the quantum field of oneness and interconnectivity to life, to your natural genius and to your inner mastery.

When you approach your golf game, leading from your right brain, you are accessing the hemisphere of your brain that operates your higher functionality. You can thank your left hemisphere for getting you to the golf course in one piece and for learning the basic mechanics of how to grip a club and how to swing. If your mechanical, linear left hemisphere is guiding your game, you can bet that you will be frustrated by your slow to nil progress. However, when you deliberately access the right hemisphere of your brain as you play—applying the self-hypnosis sessions outlined in this chapter—then you will be astounded at the ease with which you are able to enter the Zone and stay there.

In 1996, the Harvard neuroscientist Dr. Jill Bolte Taylor experienced a major stroke. At the age of 37, she could no longer read, write, walk, talk, or remember any aspect of her life. Eight years later, she completely recovered and now says she is a better version of herself. Her book, *My*

Stroke of Insight, serves as a guide for recovering brain function as it details the shutting down of her brain and her miraculous and heroic recovery.

"A healthy individual and/or society lives balanced between both halves of the brain," says Taylor. "The cause of our current state of societal imbalance is because we live 85 percent dominated by the left hemisphere, and only 15 percent from the right hemisphere. We don't just not engage the skills of the right hemisphere, we mock them!"

In other words, we shadow box with ourselves and those around us in our left-brain boxing rings, holding on with a death grip to a limited, stressful, and painful way of being. Most of us resist and refuse to avail ourselves of the fact that a much more peaceful and harmonious world is not only possible but also probable if we were to intentionally seek balance. Taylor offers, "Deep internal peace is accessible to anyone at any time. My stroke of insight would be: Peace is only a thought away, and all we have to do to access it is silence the voice of our dominating left mind."

Put simply, the Zone is always only a thought away, on or off the golf course. The only thing holding you captive to your left brain is your habitual tendency to allow it to hold you captive. And habits can be modified and changed with awareness.

What a piece of work is man—50 trillion cells functioning in purposeful harmony? The two hemispheres of our brain are yoked opposites: limit-setting rationality (time, judgment, ego) in perpetual interplay with the eternal and unbounded now. Together, and only together, do these two halves of our awareness make our human destiny.

—Jill Bolte Taylor

Preparing for the Quantum Oneness Self-Hypnosis Script

Imagine a toy top. Imagine that this top is black on top and white on the bottom. If you spin the top quickly, its color does not look black and white; it looks gray. But as the top slows down, wobbles, and eventually stops altogether, it becomes easier to see the separation between black and white.

According to Dr. John Demartini, when your energetic vibration is operating at a higher speed and a higher level, the lines of demarcation between black and white, me and you, this and that, become blurred in the whirl of joyous energy, which is when it is possible to access your natural genius and your higher guidance. It is only when the energetic vibration slows down to a near stop that "stinking thinking" happens, such as experiencing stress, being attacked by your inner critic, overthinking a shot, or being in a black-and-white or either-or point of view.

Take a moment to imagine the person with the highest, most elevated consciousness you know. This person may be religious, such as a deity, or it may be someone you know, such as a grandparent or a golf pro. Imagine that with each step you take as you walk out on the golf course, you are elevating your thoughts to the level at which this person operates. In fact, begin to associate all the walking that you do on the golf course (e.g., between holes and between shots) with elevating your consciousness to the highest, most peaceful, joyous place you can find. You might even use a walking meditation practice that you say with each step: "I awake with each step I take." Doing this will lift your awareness to a place of oneness, and the consciousness of oneness will elevate your mental game.

In the following self-hypnosis script, you will explore the concept of entering the Zone at top speed and of exploring the quantum giant you are. Enjoy!

Quantum Oneness Self-Hypnosis Script

Your Zone Golf Hypnosis Journey

Sit in a comfortable, quiet position, or recline with your head slightly elevated.

Uncross your arms and legs, and rest your hands, palms up, either by your sides or on your thighs.

Should an emergency arise at any time while in self-hypnosis, you can get up to take care of the situation simply by counting yourself up from zero to five. At five you will be wide awake, completely alert, and aware.

Close your eyes, as you nod your head slightly, signaling to your subconscious mind that you are now ready to enter into a deep state of self-hypnosis in order to radically improve your golf game. With each breath, feel a progressive relaxation move throughout your body as you begin to deeply relax. Any distracting thoughts are removed with each exhalation.

Allow a very comfortable sensation to begin to melt through your entire body, moving down through the crown of your head, gently relaxing your eyes, emptying out all the mental chatter and distracting thoughts.

With each breath, you are emptying out and letting go, becoming lighter and lighter, weightless, comfortable, and deeply relaxed.

Feel the warmth and relaxation moving down into your shoulders. As the relaxation drifts down into your hands and wrists, notice any and all residual tension, doubt, or fear emptying out through your fingertips. Take a deep breath to allow this deep release.

As you allow the relaxation to continue to move down through your chest and lungs, notice that you are filling up with a sense of spaciousness that assists you in clearing out any hardness around your heart or any limits to how great you think you are capable of being. You are now opening up completely to the natural golfing genius you truly are. Take another deep breath and feel flooded with grace, ease, and a wonderful expectancy about your next golf game.

The relaxation moves deeper down into your stomach and your lower back. You might notice a feeling of synergy among your muscles, your mind, your body, and your spirit—a connection that is working seamlessly. You are allowing your deep unconscious to support you with very clear directives about how you will play your next game at your ultimate and highest capacity.

As the relaxation drifts down, down deeper, into your pelvic area, you might notice your groin muscles relaxing, letting go, and finding their synchronicity with the rest of your power centers.

Easily and gracefully, feel the relaxation moving down through your thighs and buttocks, as a warm light makes its way down through your bones, sinews, and veins. You are continuing to become lighter still as the relaxation drifts down into your knees, calves, ankles, and feet.

As you float here, imagine that black and white top, and clearly see the separation between the white and the black. Imagine that you have the ability to spin the top as fast as it can possibly go. As you witness the blur of color, the black and white turning to gray, imagine that you can actually feel the heat coming from this top, like a whirlwind of electromagnetic energy that inspires you to spin with it. Allow your vibration to match the speed of this top, imagine that with each easy, gently relaxed breath, you are giving permission to your circuitry to operate at full tilt, at its highest frequency. Imagine that you now become a giant; this energy you are now entraining to is the same energy that is moving through your mind, heart, and body, causing you to become larger and larger with each breath you take.

Imagine now that you are a giant on the golf course, and all the hills, ponds, and putting greens are tiny compared to your enormous size and power. From the vantage point of you, a 100-foot giant, this game is like child's play. You are connected with all the power, wisdom, knowledge, grace, and awareness of the entire universe, and you are able to channel it now into this fun, human game called golf.

From your giant's perspective, imagine that you can see your little, human self standing below you way down on the golf course, midway through a game. See that this little you looks up to see the big you, that you both recognize each other, and that you realize that you are working together to have the best game possible.

See your little self receiving the power and awareness of the higher, bigger self, and as this happens, notice the feeling of connectivity to the vastness of life. See and observe the way that the little you plays golf now.

Notice the confidence, the ease, and the grace with which the little you is able to choose just the right club and maneuver the ball. (Allow a few moments of silence.)

Notice the confident way that the little you walks from one shot to the next, squaring up to the ball with a power and ease that is ten times more skilled than the task at hand requires. It is just like when you ride a bike—after years of riding, it is easy, effortless, fluid, natural, not like it used to be when you were a child first learning to ride.

See yourself taking your last putt of the day. See yourself squaring up to the ball, easily measuring the distance between the ball and the hole, and taking a deep breath as you skillfully putt the ball with the perfect amount of force. Feel the ease, grace, and satisfaction of the ball rolling right into the cup. Hear the sound, and feel the satisfaction. After you pick your ball out of the cup, take a look up, way up to the sky to acknowledge the giant version of you—you who is aware of the oneness of being. This higher, bigger self is always at hand to give you a perspective that is more powerful than anything you would find on this earth.

Contemplate the way you feel when you are connected with this giant version of yourself. Spend a few moments in the silence and try to encapsulate in a word this feeling of being connected to this power. This word might be *strength*, *power*, *confidence*, *mastery*, or *ease*. Identify this key word now.

Each and every time you desire to connect with your giant, simply lift your head to the sky. As you do, take three deep breaths while saying your key word three times. Feel the power, wisdom, and perspective of your giant infuse you with each breath.

With a smile on your face, give a nod and a silent thank-you to the giant, quantum you and know that the giant will always be there for you, whenever you need or want.

When you are ready to come back, begin counting your way back as you take a few deep breaths.

Zero—go deep asleep, quickly, soundly, and deeply, to this depth or deeper.

One—you are feeling tingly and are beginning to awaken.

Two—you are feeling emotionally calm, rested, and expanded.

Three—your feeling of well-being is flooding your entire body.

Four—you are feeling a sense that something wonderful is about to happen to you. Look for it, prepare for it, and welcome it in when it shows up.

Five—open your eyes, as you are now wide awake, alert, and aware.

Preparing for the Four-Elements Self-Hypnosis Script

The Four-Elements self-hypnosis script is designed to assist you in getting in touch with your genius nature and with nature's genius through the four elements: air, fire, earth, and water. Many shamans (or healers of power who, in tribal cultures, are considered to have a supernatural way of healing and/or producing results that ordinary people cannot access) evoke the four elements when inducing a state of transformation. Yes, golf is just a game—or is it? Perhaps what you are really endeavoring to become is the most powerful and self-actualized being you can become, to improve not only your game but also every area of your life.

In this script, you will plumb the depths of your wisdom in relation to each of the elements.

Four-Elements Self-Hypnosis Script

Your Zone Golf Hypnosis Journey

Sit in a comfortable, quiet position, or recline with your head slightly elevated.

Uncross your arms and legs, and rest your hands, palms up, either by your sides or on your thighs.

Should an emergency arise at any time while in self-hypnosis, you can get up to take care of the situation simply by counting yourself up from zero to five. At five you will be wide awake, completely alert, and aware.

Close your eyes, as you nod your head slightly, signaling to your subconscious mind that you are now ready to enter into a deep state of self-hypnosis in order to radically improve your golf game.

With each breath, feel a progressive relaxation move throughout your body as you begin to deeply relax. Any distracting thoughts are removed with each exhalation.

Begin to feel that with each breath you are melting beyond the chair or seat you are resting in, through the floorboards of the building you are contained in, through the cement, and into the ground. Begin to feel your body merging and becoming connected with the earth, like roots of a tree, extending down, down, down with each breath.

As you imagine that feeling, relaxation assists you in deepening down, down, down through your head, down deeper across your eyes, melting your face and facial muscles, your jaw going slack.

With each breath, you are emptying out and letting go, deepening down into the ground, very comfortably, like roots of a large, powerful tree, feeling safe and grounded within the soil.

The feeling sinks deeper now through your arms and fingers, like roots of relaxation that extend across your arms and fingers, feeling the power and the nurturing of the earth with each breath, as you extend deeper and deeper.

This relaxation moves all the way down through your chest, down through your spine, as you allow yourself to feel deeply grounded and anchored, in sync and in rhythm with the earth. This sensation continues to move down through your navel, and you feel an expanding umbilical cord move from your naval into branches of roots. This umbilical cord extends down into the soil, and you feel the oxygen of the earth feeding you and nurturing you. Become aware of the rich smell and the safe, powerful feeling of nurturing in your core.

The sensation is now deepening down into your hips and pelvic area and is lowering now through your legs. It continues to move all the way down through your toes and through the soles of your feet. It extends out through the soles of your feet and is dropping down, down, down into the soil. It now moves deeper down to the core of the earth, to the essence of all creation. Imagine with your next deep breath that the root extensions that emanate from your fingers, toes, and umbilical cord embed themselves here in the core of the earth and create a permanent bond.

Feel the roots from your body extending to adhere to the core of the earth in such a way that they can never be severed. (Allow a few moments of silence as you feel this connection taking place.)

Take three deep breaths and feel the power that you are now connected with. Feel this strength and power inform each of your cells, atoms, bones, fibers, organs, and all functions of your human body temple.

You are now deeply and forever at one with the movement and with the subtleties of the earth: the crevices, mounds, hills, valleys, flowers, trees, and every blade of grass.

Imagine now the golf course that you will be playing on, and imagine that you are now connected beneath the golf course. You understand on a deep level the under and inner workings of this course. You feel that the course is not separate from you but an extension of you. You know it like the back of your own hand.

With a deep appreciation of your new connection with the world and life that underlie the golf course, from a root level, ask the earth what it has to teach you. Allow the earth to impart a message to you regarding your golf game—a secret from deep within that will assist you in improving your game from the inside out. (Allow a few moments of silence as you contemplate this.)

As you embody this message from deep within the earth, know that, right now, each and every time you touch the grass, whether you pick up your golf ball or wipe off your club face, you will be reminded about this message from earth, and you will revisit this feeling of being grounded and at one with the earth. You recall the feelings of being at one with the vast matrix that constitutes the golf course, and you feel as familiar with the course as you are with your breathing—even if it is your first time golfing on a particular course.

As you are now deeply connected with the core of the earth, begin to feel the molten lava from the center of the earth. As if you were peering into a deep volcano, imagine and feel the heat and hear the bubbling of the lava fire, but know that you remain unafraid and unable to be hurt in any way.

Feel the deep passion of this lava fire, erupting from deep within. Feel the energy as it rises to the surface in an exhilarated celebration: a fountain that lifts you up in celebration.

Feel the ecstasy of this lava fire; it's like the exhilaration you feel when you tee off and make perfect contact with the golf ball, hitting the ball long and straight to your desired spot on the golf course.

Continue to marvel and explore this fiery substance that escalates your passion for your golf game, your desire to improve and take the necessary action to become better day after day.

Ask the fire what its message is for you. What is the gift or the secret message from the fire that will assist you in your golf game? (Allow a few moments of silence as you contemplate this.)

As you embody this fiery wisdom into your blood and your DNA, feel passionate and excited about being alive. Contemplate your next golf game, and know that as you play and feel the warmth of the sun, you will be reminded of the fire that resides within you, of your passion, the vitality that animates you, and the gift or message that you received from the element of fire.

Allow this lava to elevate you, and give thanks for it as you take its strength with you and begin to lift and rise up from the center of the earth, lifting and rising but maintaining your connection with the depth of your earthly and fiery nature. With each breath, you are rising higher above the ground, like a volcano that erupts—higher and higher until you explode and then comfortably land in the tall branches of a nearby tree.

Feel the power of the fire and the sturdiness of the earth below you, still very much alive in you while you are resting atop a very high branch, miles above the earth below. Begin to feel the coolness of the air up here, the peacefulness, wisdom, detachment, freedom, and greater perspective.

Imagine now that a large bird, perhaps an eagle, lands next to you on the tall branch. It invites you to climb on its back so that you can see the world from its perspective. You see that it is large enough to easily carry you on its back, so you take a deep breath and climb aboard.

The eagle begins to flap its majestic wings and carries you through the air, transporting you gracefully and smoothly through the air. You and the eagle fly together higher and higher, from glory to greater glory. You feel completely safe on the back of this powerful eagle: you feel the wind on your face, and the sun warming your head, neck, and back.

Take a look at the golf course miles below and see how tiny it is from way up here. Notice the golfers below and how simple each shot looks from your heightened perspective. It is as if you can easily see the simplest way to hit and putt each hole—everything becomes basic and simple from way up here. With the next three breaths, breathe in the qualities of wisdom and simplicity that come from a higher, objective view.

Your eagle has a particular message or gift to impart to you that will give you an edge in your golf game. What is it? Become willing and receptive with each breath to allow your eagle to communicate with you. Take a couple of breaths as you identify what the message or gift is. Once you've identified what this message is, breathe it in to your heart and soul as you allow each cell of your body to breathe in the message. The potency of the message begins to work with you on a cellular level, rearranging and reorganizing your assemblage point, bringing you to greater awareness and clarity and freedom. Take a big, deep breath as you lock in this powerful message.

See that your eagle is flying with you, getting closer and closer to earth—moving in the direction of a beautiful lake. The eagle glides in gracefully and easily, assisting you to a soft patch of green grass alongside this beautiful, crystal-blue lake. You thank your eagle for sharing its wisdom with you and for taking you on this journey through the air.

Each and every time you are on the golf course and feel a breeze or become aware of a bird flying overhead, you will be reminded of your ability to see things from a higher view and of the message or gift from your eagle. You are reminded to breathe deeply and to connect with your natural state of freedom that allows you to fly and soar into success in your golf game.

With all this traveling, you must be thirsty, so take a drink of the clean, clear water from the pristine lake. Feel the refreshment as the sweet water washes against the back of your throat and gently moves its way down your throat. As the water glides down your throat, notice how quickly it cools and quenches your thirst.

Watch the ripples on the water, which move all the way across the lake as you touch and drink from its abundant source. As you feel the warmth of the sun on your head, shoulders, and back, feel the desire for refreshment as you prepare to swim in this beautiful lake. As you step in one foot at a time or dive in from the grassy edge, feel each body part drink in the sweetness of the lake. Feel the relief, the vitality, the aliveness of your body being able to float and swim safely, easily, and comfortably in this lake. As if the lake were the fountain of youth, you notice your body being transformed by this water, rejuvenated, and made new.

Feel the wisdom of the lake speak to you—watch how the water moves around the rocks and shows you the true meaning of flow, ease, grace, and fluidity. Begin to contemplate your golf swing, and see yourself swinging the club easily, gently, gracefully, and seamlessly. You are completely connected to the intertwined position of your hands on the club; the pivot in your feet; and the movement of your hips, shoulders, and head.

Feel and imagine that you are all water (science shows that human bodies comprise at least 70 percent water), and feel the wisdom of the water within you as the water embraces you. Feel the dance of unity. Feel the wisdom; feel the ease and relaxation. You intuitively know how to let go and flow. Each and every time you find yourself tensing up during a golf game, you will automatically remember the element of water and you will instantly relax and access the brilliance that is always flowing within you.

Right now, ask the water what gift it has for you. What is the special message it has for you to assist you in your golf game. Ask the water to reveal it to you now. (Allow a few moments of silence as you connect with this message.)

As you take the next few breaths, absorb the secret that the water has to share with you as a sponge would. Each and every time you see a body of water, you will be reminded to relax, to enjoy the game, and to allow yourself to be fluid in your strokes and as you move through your game. And each and every time you see water or drink its refreshing substance, you will be reminded of your inherent power, grace, and fluidity as you move through life, on and off the golf course.

Recall your triggers of the elements. Each and every time you touch grass, whether to pick up your golf ball or to clean off your tee, you are reminded of your message from earth. You revisit this feeling of being grounded, of being at one with the vast matrix of the golf course, and you feel as familiar with the course as you do with your breathing—even if it is your first time golfing on a particular course.

Each and every time you are playing golf and you feel the heat of the sun warming your head, face, or shoulders, you will be reminded of the fire that resides within you, of your passion and the vitality that animates you. The heat of the sun fills you with excitement about your game and about the progress you are making.

Each and every time you are on the golf course and you feel a breeze (or see a bird fly overhead), you are reminded of your ability to see things from a higher perspective. You will be reminded to breathe deeply and to connect with your natural freedom that allows you to fly and soar into greater and greater success with your golf game.

Each and every time you see a body of water, you will be reminded to relax, to enjoy the moment, and to allow yourself to be fluid in your game. Each and every time you see water or drink it, you will be reminded of your power, grace, and the fluid way you are capable of moving through life, on and off the golf course.

In the next few moments, you will begin to count yourself back from zero to five. Take a few deep breaths.

Zero—you go deep asleep, quickly, soundly, deeply to this depth or deeper.

One—feel physically rejuvenated as you are beginning to awaken.

Two—notice a feeling of calm as you feel rested and expanded.

Three—allow a feeling of well-being to flood your entire being as you sense your connection to all the elements that surround you and make it possible for you to enjoy your golf game in a holistic way.

Four—feel that you are supported by the four elements.

Five—now allow your eyes to open, as you feel wide awake, alert, aware, and great.

Preparing for the Scorecard Self-Hypnosis Script

I have a tip that can take five strokes off anyone's golf game: it's called an eraser.

—*Arnold Palmer*

The Zone Golf scorecard self-hypnosis script will help you to make the vastness of the quantum oneness and all the elements you've been exploring something tangible, tactile, and earth bound. In this self-hypnosis script, you will be reframing the way you relate to your golf scorecard. On a blank piece of paper, write "Zone Golf Scorecard" at the top. Next, number from 1 to 9 or from 1 to 18 (the number of holes you played on your last game) across the top. Along the left side write the following list:

- yards
- par
- score

- putts
- good shots
- drives on the fairway
- number of greens in regulation
- mistakes
- hazards
- number of out of bounds
- corrected mistakes
- total points

Zone Golf Scorecard

	1	2	3	4	5	6	7	8	9
Yards	362	187	523	371	365	535	405	156	329
Par	4	3	5	4	4	5	4	3	4
Score	6	4	5	5	6	8	6	6	5
Putts	2	3	3	3	3	2	2	1	3
Good shots	2	3	3	3	3	2	2	1	3
Drives on the fairway	1		1			1	1		1
Greens in regulation		1	1	1		1		1	
Mistakes	3	2	3	2	5	5	4	5	3
Hazards	1							1	
# of OBs								1	
Corrected mistakes	3	2	3	2	5	5	4	5	3

Qualities I expressed in my game today were: patience, confidence, appreciation, improvement, commitment, passion, focus, concentration, willingness

Total good shots:	1 x <u>19</u> = 19	
Total mistakes:	2 x <u>32</u> = 64	
Total corrected mistakes:	3 x <u>32</u> = 96	
Total qualities:	5 x <u>9</u> = 45	

TOTAL SCORE = <u>184</u>

Review your most recent golf game. Once you've input the yardage, par, and score, give yourself a point for each good shot (i.e., the drives, shots, and putts that you did well), two points for every mistake you made, and three points for every corrected mistake you made. For example, if you overshot a hole on the green and then replayed the shot in your mind's eye, give yourself two points. If you took a moment to imagine doing it again, using less force and more control, seeing the ball roll with just the right speed into the hole, then give yourself three points for that corrected mistake. The name of the game is to allow the space for greater freedom, greater self-expression, and ultimately an improved game. To do this, you must reframe the way you think of mistakes. Instead of trying to get the lowest score possible, as you play using the Zone Golf scorecard, the name of your game is to get the most points. The more points you get on your Zone Golf scorecard, the lower your actual golf score will become and the more progress you will be making toward golfing in the Zone.

There is a space for you to acknowledge the qualities and virtues you expressed during the game on your scorecard. It is one thing to acknowledge that you did something well, but it takes it to a higher level when you recognize what the action or behavior means about you and your character. Some examples of qualities you might experience out on the golf course are patience, confidence, appreciation, improvement, commitment, passion, focus, concentration, willingness, and peacefulness. Give yourself five points on your Zone Golf scorecard for each quality you expressed in your game.

Make sure you begin the following self-hypnosis session with your

Zone Golf scorecard and pen or pencil in hand to keep track of your points. The more often you review this script, the more you will be training your subconscious to look for all the things you currently do right. And you are also learning not only to embrace mistakes but also to look forward to them for the inherent growth and learning opportunities that they provide.

Zone Golf Scorecard Self-Hypnosis Script

Your Zone Golf Hypnosis Journey

Sit in a comfortable, quiet position, or recline with your head slightly elevated.

Uncross your arms and legs, and rest your hands, palms up, either by your sides or on your thighs.

Should an emergency arise at any time while in self-hypnosis, you can get up to take care of the situation simply by counting yourself up from zero to five. At five you will be wide awake, completely alert, and aware.

Close your eyes and nod your head slightly, signaling to your subconscious mind that you are ready to enter a deep state of self-hypnosis to radically improve your golf game.

As you begin, take a few very deep breaths, and you may begin to notice certain parts of your body relaxing. Perhaps other parts are still a little tense. Just become aware of this, as your body continues to relax— the way your clothes feel on your body, the way the air feels as it gently brushes up against your face.

Notice your body being completely supported by the weight of the chair, couch, bed, or whatever it is that is holding you up.

As you read this, become aware of how good it feels to breathe in deeply and slowly, and to release completely. Feel your chest and stomach rise with each inhalation, and contract with each exhalation. Notice the release and the letting go that takes place now. With each breath that you exhale, you release all your cares of the day.

With each breath you breathe out, you let go of any and all tension that may linger in your body. And with each and every inhalation, you breathe in a sense of peace and relaxation.

Begin to count yourself down into a deeper state of relaxation. Start with five and move down to zero. At zero you will go deep asleep, a receptive state of focused relaxation. And with each count, you become more and more relaxed, and completely peaceful.

Begin with five, as you let go with each breath.

Four—all tension washes away.

Three—allow yourself to feel heavy in the chair or on whatever surface holds you up.

Two—let go more than before, as you prepare yourself to discover an inner resourcefulness that will improve the way you approach your golf game and relate to yourself as a golfer.

One—prepare to enter the Zone.

· Zero—deep asleep. Each and every time you read or hear "deep asleep," you go quickly, soundly, and deeply to this depth or deeper for the purpose of entering the Zone and radically transforming your mental golf game.

With the next few breaths, I'm going to ask you to revisit your most recent golf game. And you may be holding your real or imagined Zone Golf scorecard in your hand, which is a different kind of scorecard than you are used to. With this scorecard, you get a point for each thing you do right, two points for every mistake you make, and three points for every corrected mistake (that you correct in your mind's eye). The name of the game is to get the most points. The more points you get, the more progress you are making toward becoming a Zone golfer.

Regardless of how well you did or didn't do, acknowledge yourself for getting out there. As you review your last game, call to mind all that you did right on each hole. How did you swing? How did you putt? Go through each hole and give yourself a point for each of your good shots. Don't be stingy with yourself. Give credit where credit is due. (Allow a few minutes for this process to unfold.)

Now take the next few minutes and praise yourself for what you did right and what that must mean about you. For example,

- You got up in the morning despite the fact that you were tired and it was cold outside: you are dedicated (one point).
- Your first tee shot of the day was powerful and went straight to where you wanted it to go: you are focused (one point).
- You made a delicate chip shot from deep grass to a close-cut pin on the fourth hole: you are masterful (one point).
- You congratulated your teammate when he or she made a birdie with a series of great shots: you are supportive (one point).

- Your swing on the tenth hole was the strongest it has ever been: you are improving and getting stronger (one point).
- You played eighteen holes today: you are vital, active, and agile (one point).
- You were able to dedicate several hours to your golf game: you are lucky (one point).
- You recognized the beauty of the manicured grass, the elegant ponds, and the rows of flowers: you are appreciative (one point).

Now take a few minutes of silence and contemplate all the good shots you made. Add them up, hole by hole, and write them down on your Zone Golf scorecard. (Allow a few minutes for this process.)

Now, take a couple of moments to acknowledge the areas that were challenging, where your concentration may have lapsed, and where you made mistakes. This is an opportunity not to bludgeon yourself but to simply acknowledge the areas in which you would have liked to have done better—give yourself a point for each of these shots. Now, see yourself replaying those shots in your mind, the way you would have liked to have played them. As you go through each shot, one at a time, give yourself three points for each corrected mistake.

Yes, in this scorecard, even if you made a mistake, if you go back and correct it, it counts as three points, and the more points the better. Now do this for every hole. And when you are done, add up your total points.

At this point, you see that you've been a huge success today. You are right on target, becoming stronger, clearer, and more focused, and enjoying your golf game more and more. Each day, in every way, the

Zone is becoming a moment-to-moment reality for you. Your feeling of well-being is becoming stronger and stronger with every breath you take. Repeat this process after each game to create a tangible way to track your progress. I even suggest that you take your Zone Golf scorecard to the golf course with you and fill it in simultaneously with your ordinary golf scorecard. If you do this, after a short period of time, you will notice that, as your Zone Golf scorecard numbers increase, your golf score decreases.

In a few moments, count yourself awake, from zero to five. At zero, you'll go deep asleep, deeper than ever before. At five, you'll be wide awake, alert, and aware, and you'll feel great.

Acknowledge yourself for having taken this time for yourself, for filling in your Zone Golf scorecard, and for giving yourself the gift of taking control of your life. You are doing something that will help you achieve more success not only in your golf game but also in your daily life.

Make an inner commitment to yourself to work with your Zone Golf scorecard for at least the remainder of the 28-day program to reinforce the mental habits you are creating, then nod your head right now as a signal to your subconscious mind that you are in sync.

Very good. Take three deep breaths as you prepare to come back.

Zero—deep asleep. Go deep asleep, quickly, soundly, deeply to this depth or deeper.

One—notice that you feel physically relaxed, are beginning to awaken, and feel pleased with yourself for how well you scored on your Zone Golf scorecard.

Two—feel emotionally calm, rested, and expanded. Feel successful and inspired to play your next round of golf.

Three—a feeling of well-being washes over your entire body, as the color of success encodes itself within you.

Four—become aware that something wonderful is happening to you. Acknowledge yourself for all the great work you have been doing and all that you will continue to do.

Five—open your eyes. You are wide awake, completely alert, and aware, and feeling great.

Secret Takeaways

- Deep internal peace is accessible to anyone at any time.
- You get more of what you focus on.

ZONE IN

Your natural golfing genius already resides within you

The way in is the way out.

—Rev. Michael Beckwith

Secret Synopsis

Just as the blueprint for the mighty oak tree resides within the acorn, your natural golfing genius already resides within you. This chapter will assist you in entering the Zone and connecting with your inner golf pro via music as you create your own one-of-a-kind Zone Golf soundtrack.

Your Personalized Zone Golf Soundtrack

Call to mind one of your favorite pieces of music. Can you identify the feelings that the song or melody evokes? Does it make you feel happy, inspired, free, victorious, invigorated, or sentimental? One of the reasons we humans love music so much is not just because it enlivens us or inspires us or enhances our ability to connect with deep emotions and cherished memories, but because rhythm is integral to the human body (i.e., our heartbeat, our breathing, our walking pace). The fact that music is an organizing force to align the body, mind, and spirit is why music has become the secret weapon of some professional golfers, including Vijay Singh. In fact, some professional golfers won't step foot on a golf course without their lucky MP3 player in hand that is loaded with their personal golf playlist to help them smooth out their swing.

We have all heard the saying, "Music calms the savage beast." It has been proven that music is one of the quickest ways to shift your state of mind and to put you in the Zone. Dating all the way back to 428 BC, Socrates, Plato, and Aristotle so recognized music's ability to affect behavior and stimulate higher thinking that music became the hub around which their teaching curricula revolved. Research also proves that different types of music affect people uniquely. My husband, Dana Walden, was part of a project that conducted scientific studies to determine what type of music was best for putting a person into the alpha and theta states. What the scientists discovered was that music that relaxed one person stressed another person out, and what put one person in the Zone could agitate another. The bottom line is that each human is unique, and it is your job to determine the music that will help you access the Zone most effectively.

Your homework for this chapter is to create your Zone Golf soundtrack. You and only you can determine the music that helps you to bypass the maze of your mind and put you into that state of ultimate well-being, where you can access your natural genius.

Because the golf swing is rhythmic, you are on the hunt for music that matches the unique beat of your inner drum. Some people swing as fast as a merengue beat; some people swing in time with a waltz. Once you discover your unique swing tempo, and play it while you are on the golf course, you will enter the Zone more easily, more reliably, and more quickly.

As you no doubt have experienced, listening to music is an amazing way to cease your mind's chatter and to drown out disruptive sounds around you. If, for example, the banter among other players on the seventh hole serves as a distraction for you, bring your own MP3 player to the golf course. When you pop your ear buds into place, their lips will be moving but you, gratefully, will have no idea what they are saying.

Now, if you are the social type and want to be engaged in constant dialogue with your fellow golfers, then this might not be the technique for you. However, if you are playing alone, try the Zone Golf soundtrack to see the difference it can make in your ability to maintain access to the Zone.

The Zone Golf Soundtrack

The way to find the Zone Golf soundtrack that is perfect for you will take some experimenting. Search for songs that will put you in the optimum state for the following actions:

- Traveling to the course (e.g., "Bright Side of the Road," Van Morrison)
- Walking out to the putting green ("What a Wonderful World," Michael Bublé)

- Swinging ("Bamboleo," Gypsy Kings)
- Teeing off ("Pachelbel's Canon," Angels of Venice)
- Taking fairway shots ("Unwritten," Natasha Bedingfield)
- Putting ("Somewhere over the Rainbow," Israel Kamakawiwo'ole)
- Idling while your companions play or walking between holes ("Gotta Be," Des'ree)
- Returning to the Zone if you get distracted or hit a ball into a bunker ("Keeping the Faith," Billy Joel)
- Leaving the course ("My Way," Frank Sinatra)

Zone Golf Tempo Track

On www.sourcebooks.com/extras/zonegolf, I've included a music-only track to set the tempo and that you can put on repeat play to get you started with your Zone Golf soundtrack.

Listen to this tempo track while practicing your swing. If the tempo feels too fast or too slow for you, then consider yourself one step closer to finding the tempo that is right for you.

Listening to the tempo track takes practice, so I suggest that you spend a couple of hours practicing swinging with the track before you actually play a game with it. If you want the track to play continuously, then set your MP3 player to a repeat or continuous play setting.

Once you decide on your Zone Golf soundtrack and become accustomed to the tracks that work best for certain shots, after a while, you will be able to enter the Zone and remain there, on demand, and to exponentially increase your effectiveness on the golf course.

Creating Your Zone Golf Soundtrack

Discovering the rest of your Zone Golf soundtrack will increase your focus by drowning out the commotion and chatter of the other players around you. As you listen to your Zone Golf playlist, your body will synchronize with the beat of the music, connecting you with your natural rhythm and smoothing out your swing.

The remainder of your Zone Golf playlist should be as unique as you are: it should contain music that uplifts your one-of-a-kind spirit, whether that be country, jazz, hard rock, rap, or instrumental. Once you have your Zone Golf playlist, you will need to practice golfing with it, as it will take some getting used to. The practice will be well worth it, though, because with your Zone Golf soundtrack you will be a more relaxed, happier golfer as you strike the ball with more consistency and precision.

Here are some guidelines for creating your playlist:

- To find the sweet spot and put you into that perfect swing Zone for teeing off, discover the tempo that matches your groove. I suggest the Zone Golf tempo track. If that doesn't work for you, try something with a Latin beat (e.g., Gypsy Kings).
- For fairway shots, listen to something inspirational (e.g., the *Rocky* theme).
- For putts or difficult shots, try a calming instrumental (e.g., Stephen Halpern's "Chakra Balancing").
- For bunker shots or to cheer up, try a song that is uplifting (e.g., "My Girl," by Smokey Robinson, or "Take It Easy," by the Eagles).

- As you leave the golf course, play something inspiring and victorious as a pat on the back for getting out there and giving it your best ("I Believe I Can Fly," by R. Kelly).

If you think that bringing an MP3 player to the golf course complete with your Zone Golf soundtrack seems ridiculous, think about what Einstein said: "You can't solve a problem with the same mind that created it." To create the transformational results you desire and deserve, you have to take risks and think outside the box.

Song Suggestions for Your Zone Golf Playlist

Driving to the Golf Course

"Centerfield," John Fogerty

"Let's Get Lost," Chet Baker

"I Hope You Dance," Lee Ann Womack

"Anticipation," Carly Simon

Teeing Off

Zone Golf Tempo Track

"Bamboleo" or "Volare," Gypsy Kings

"Celebration," Kool and the Gang

"One Love," Bob Marley

"Eye of the Tiger," Survivor

"A Feeling Like That," Gary Allan

"Dance to the Music," Sly and the Family Stone

"Everybody Is a Star," Sly and the Family Stone

"Dreams Can Come True," Gabrielle

Fairway Shots

"Sunshine on My Shoulders," John Denver

"Gotta Be," Des'ree

"Jump," Van Halen

"The River," Garth Brooks

"Unwritten," Natasha Bedingfield

"Seasons of Love," from *Rent*

"Fields of Gold," Eva Cassidy (or Sting)

"Heaven Is a Place on Earth," Belinda Carlisle

"Walking on Sunshine," Katrina and the Waves

"Rainbow Connection," Kermit the Frog

Hazard Shots

"The Best Is Yet to Come," Frank Sinatra

"You Raise Me Up," Josh Groban

"Calling All Angels," Train

"You Learn," Alanis Morissette

"Somewhere over the Rainbow," Israel Kamakawiwo'ole

"Keeping the Faith," Billy Joel

"The Prayer of St. Francis," Skye Dyer

"Coming Out of the Dark," Gloria Estefan

"Reach," Gloria Estefan

"Stand," Rascal Flatts

"Angel," Sarah McLachlan

"It's Hard to Be Humble," Mac Davis

Putts

"How 'Bout Us," Wk.end Band

"The Mission," Ennio Morricone

"Encantado," Music of the Pink Dolphins

"Chakra Balancing," Stephen Halpern

"Pachelbel's Canon," Angels of Venice

"Shepherd Moons" and "Paint the Sky with Stars," Enya

Driving Home

"My Way," Frank Sinatra

"Life Is Wonderful," Jason Mraz

"The River of Dreams," Billy Joel

"Take Me Home," Phil Collins

"What a Wonderful World," Louis Armstrong

"100 Years," Five for Fighting

"Thank You," Dido

"Thank U," Alanis Morissette

"The Living Years," Mike and the Mechanics

"What a Wonderful World," Michael Bublé

"I'm Still Standing," Elton John

"I Still Haven't Found What I'm Looking For," U2

"Back in the High Life," Steve Winwood

"Imagine," John Lennon

Preparing for the Zone-In Self-Hypnosis Script

In this session, you will be creating a strong inner reference point to anchor yourself in the Zone. To appreciate the value of an inner reference point, it might be helpful to identify its opposite.

It is human nature to have our outer reference points rule our attention and well-being. Examples of outer reference points are the weather, the economy, horoscopes, the promotion we got or didn't get at work, and of course our golf score. All of those things are outer reference points by which we benchmark how well we are doing in life, whether we are happy or sad, triumphant or depressed.

Most of us do not realize that as human beings we are endogenous creatures. Something that is endogenous is caused by factors inside an organism or system. Most people think that they are the product of their environment, in the same way that they consider a palm tree to be indigenous to a particular climate. Take a palm tree out of a tropical place such as Florida and repot it in the Arctic, and it will have a difficult time surviving.

Human beings are certainly influenced by their surroundings, but ultimately humans are endogenous: we are capable of creating our own inner climate regardless of the physical or psychological weather around us.

For example, it is possible that everything is going wrong, it is raining, you've just had a fight with your spouse, you just got a flat tire, and you shanked the ball on the first tee. Yet if you are able to Zone in (return your attention to your inner reference point), there is no reason you can't turn the beat around and play the best game of your life. Whether or not you do is a matter of where you place your attention.

Instead of being ruled by what people think of you, the following self-hypnosis script will help you to root yourself in the Zone regardless of rain and which way the wind is blowing.

Zone-In Self-Hypnosis Script

Your Zone Golf Hypnosis Journey

Sit in a comfortable, quiet position, or recline with your head slightly elevated.

Uncross your arms and legs, and rest your hands, palms up, either by your sides or on your thighs.

Should an emergency arise at any time while in self-hypnosis, you can get up to take care of the situation simply by counting yourself up from zero to five. At five you will be wide awake, completely alert, and aware.

Close your eyes and nod your head slightly, signaling to your subconscious mind that you are ready to enter a deep state of self-hypnosis to radically improve your golf game.

As you begin, take a few very deep breaths, and you may begin to notice certain parts of your body relaxing. Perhaps other parts are still a little tense. Just become aware of this, as your body continues to relax—the way your clothes feel on your body, the way the air feels as it gently brushes up against your face.

Notice your body being completely supported by the weight of the chair, couch, bed, or whatever it is that is holding you up.

As you read this, become aware of how good it feels to breathe in deeply and slowly, and to release completely. Feel your chest and stomach rise with each inhalation, and contract with each exhalation. Notice the release and the letting go that takes place now. With each breath that you exhale, you release all your cares of the day.

With each breath you breathe out, you let go of any and all tension that may linger in your body. And with each and every inhalation, you breathe in a sense of peace and relaxation.

Begin to count yourself down into a deeper state of relaxation. Start with five and move down to zero. At zero you will go deep asleep, a receptive state of focused relaxation. And with each count, you become more and more relaxed, and completely peaceful.

Begin with five, as you let go with each breath.

Four—all tension washes away.

Three—allow yourself to feel heavy in the chair or on whatever surface holds you up.

Two—let go more than before, as you prepare yourself to discover an inner resourcefulness that will improve the way you approach your golf game and relate to yourself as a golfer.

One—prepare to enter the Zone.

Zero—deep asleep. Each and every time you read or hear "deep asleep," you go quickly, soundly, and deeply to this depth or deeper for the purpose of entering the Zone and radically transforming your mental golf game.

Imagine that you are now taking a tour of your inner being so that you can gain a glimpse of your best self. Your best self is the you who you would be if you got completely out of your own way and actualized your fullest potential and gifts.

Begin by zoning in on your right toe. Feel the glow, the tingle, and the genius of your toe. Now, notice its perfect alignment with your right foot. Imagine your entire right foot perfectly placed on the green. Feel the way your feet feel as they are solidly grounded when you tee off, when you putt, or when you walk from one hole to the next. Notice the specific way that you feel when you are standing in alignment with your highest self.

Imagine this light as it is moving from your toe, through your feet, and up into your ankles, glowing as it moves into the muscles of your calves.

Feel the perfect balance of musculature, agility, ease, and strength as this light moves up now into your shins and into your knees. Feel the wisdom of your knees—the way they automatically bend and lift to align your body perfectly as you swing and putt.

The light begins to move gradually upward through your thighs. Feel the bones, tendons, and muscles powerfully in sync with the intelligence of the whole of your body.

Move the light of your best self up through your pelvic area and your hips. Feel the strength, flexibility, and genius of your hips, the way they connect radiantly with your torso, stomach, and lower back. Feel all these groups of muscles operating in synergy with your unique genius code. See and feel the way your body maneuvers, one muscle group at a time, in slow motion, swinging, putting, and hitting the ball.

All the physical practice you've done and all the mental practice are now integrated within you. This integration takes place as the light moves its way up through every cell, every atom, every fiber of each muscle, organ, heartbeat, breath, and even every space between each breath.

Notice this resonance move up into your chest and heart; feel your lungs breathe deeply in and deeply out, resonant with the intelligence within you. All of the many clusters of muscles are orchestrated together into one seamless genius stroke.

Envision your body as if you were looking through a high-powered microscope. Watch in awe at the complex mystery of creation that you are: perfectly organized to perform at maximum efficiency, elegance, and precision on and off the golf course. Feel your heart open wide—wider than you thought it could. With every breath you take, feel the expansion of your lungs and the expansion of your heart.

This flood of well-being supports you organically as it moves upward through your neck and head. Witness with awe the effortless position of your head as your neck cradles it. Become aware of the complex bundles of nerves and synapses that operate synergistically, without you having to think about them.

Light now moves up into your head. Feel and sense the optimum expression of all the systems of your brain. Imagine now that you can travel an inner stairwell up through the neurons of your brain. Behold the synapses firing when your brain is operating at maximum efficiency and productivity. Move within the interior of your nose, ears, and eyes to the uppermost region of your mind.

Imagine that you have entered a crystalline dome that has a ceiling that allows you to see out into infinity. It is here that you glimpse your greatest possibilities.

Most people don't even know that this place exists within them. But now you do. Most people access only 12 percent of the mind's power. But now you have access to 100 percent of your mind's power. It is as if you were in a field of diamonds twinkling in the sun. Feel the heat and energy of this higher region of your mind's power and feel that it is open to even higher influence through the skylight of your mind.

From here it is easy to see that there is no limit to what you are capable of. Thus far, you have been observing the way your body looks and feels when it is functioning at peak efficiency, or when you are in the Zone. But the truth is that the Zone is not a static state. It is dynamic, ever changing, moving, and expanding, just as you are.

From this vantage point, you begin to see that the Zone is the entry point to the vastness of your capabilities—as a golfer and as a spiritual being with a human experience.

Feel the influence of being aware of your connection to this higher intelligence, beyond simply playing well or beating your score from the day before.

For the following 30 seconds, allow yourself to be flooded with this sunlight from a higher plane. Allow yourself to bask in this brightness, this levity, this buoyancy, this new and improved version of who you are and what you are capable of on and off the golf course.

Recognize that your mind contains the intelligence that governs all the thousands of muscles that are upgrading, even as you read this. Allow yourself, in these next few moments of silence, to integrate this upgraded way of being. (Allow a few moments of silence.)

Now imagine arriving at the golf course fully organized in this new awareness. Before you get out of your car, you Zone in: you imagine travel through your body, beginning with your left toe and working your way up until you can see yourself in absolute perfection, the way you most desire to be, the way you actually are as your highest self.

Travel this journey all the way until you get to the crown of your head, the control center, and feel the skylight open to receive divine guidance, higher wisdom that floods throughout your entire body. Now you are in a dynamic state, your ultimate state of being and golfing—in other words, you are in the Zone.

See yourself getting out of your car, glowing, walking as if your feet barely touched the ground, but you feel completely grounded. See yourself position your body to tee off. Notice how gracefully and easily you maneuver your body in alignment. Become aware of what you say to yourself. Notice whether there is any mental noise. Can you feel this pronounced state of well-being?

Now notice your next shot, the confidence, the joy, the ease, and the alignment of your body, mind, and spirit. All the many aspects of your physical body are now operating harmoniously.

See yourself at the second hole, smiling, enjoying, and relishing this great experience. Now note what is absent. Stress, worry, or hurry? You might try to play the way you used to play, but the more you try, the more impossible it is—once you expand your ways, it is impossible to shrink back to your former way of being. Welcome to your new benchmark.

See yourself finishing up your game. You are glowing, smiling, and feeling grateful for how far you've come and how great you are doing. Allow a feeling of gratitude to well up within you for all the many miracles that occur in your body temple.

From this moment forward, each and every time you want to Zone in to amplify and accelerate your capability as a golfer, simply say "Zone in." Say "Zone in" to yourself while taking three deep breaths, and you will go to this depth or deeper. This is your new set point.

With gratitude, take three deep breaths and begin to move from zero to five. Zero represents deep asleep, deeper than before, and five represents wide awake, completely awake, and aware.

Zero—deep asleep, deeper than before.

One—you feel physically relaxed but inspired.

Two—you feel emotionally calm, peaceful, and happy to know that each and every time you Zone in, your inner reference point is becoming stronger and stronger and your golf game is continuously improving.

Three—elevate, and become aware of the air on your skin. Slightly move your fingers and toes to signal that you are about to awaken. You are now integrating your inner reference point deep into your subconscious mind.

Four—move your awareness to this level by taking a big, deep breath as a feeling of well-being washes over you.

Five—open your eyes, and you are wide awake. You are now completely awake and aware, and feeling great.

Preparing for the Self-Hypnosis Script for Becoming the Golf Pro You Are

The following self-hypnosis script will help you identify a golfer whom you greatly admire and then emulate, become, and integrate the aspect of him or her that is within you. As you do this, you will activate and enliven the pro within you, thus elevating yourself, mentally, and ultimately physically to a higher standard.

Self-Hypnosis Script for Becoming the Golf Pro You Are

Your Zone Golf Hypnosis Journey

Sit in a comfortable, quiet position, or recline with your head slightly elevated.

Uncross your arms and legs, and rest your hands, palms up, either by your sides or on your thighs.

Should an emergency arise at any time while in self-hypnosis, you can get up to take care of the situation simply by counting yourself up from zero to five. At five you will be wide awake, completely alert, and aware.

Close your eyes and nod your head slightly, signaling to your subconscious mind that you are ready to enter a deep state of self-hypnosis to radically improve your golf game.

As you begin, take a few very deep breaths, and you may begin to notice certain parts of your body relaxing. Perhaps other parts are still a little tense. Just become aware of this, as your body continues to relax—the way your clothes feel on your body, the way the air feels as it gently brushes up against your face.

Notice your body being completely supported by the weight of the chair, couch, bed, or whatever it is that is holding you up.

As you read this, become aware of how good it feels to breathe in deeply and slowly, and to release completely. Feel your chest and stomach rise with each inhalation, and contract with each exhalation. Notice the release and the letting go that takes place now. With each breath that you exhale, you release all your cares of the day.

With each breath you breathe out, you let go of any and all tension that may linger in your body. And with each and every inhalation, you breathe in a sense of peace and relaxation.

Right now, you have permission to be fully present, despite anything else that may be going on in your life. All thoughts and concerns are released with each breath, leaving you replenished, relaxed, deeper and deeper with each and every deep breath.

On your next deep inhale hold it for a count of eight. Eight, seven, six, five, four, three, two, one, and release completely. Now hold the next breath in for a count of six—six, five, four, three, two, one. Very good. Now four—four, three, two, one. And now bring your breath back to its natural rhythm.

In this relaxed state, your subconscious mind is more readily available to bask in the positive suggestions you are about to receive. With this next breath, give thanks for your amazing subconscious mind—that part of you that is responsible for transformation and growth. You can also think of your subconscious mind as the 88 percent that controls the buttons, switches, and levers of your mind's power.

Begin to count from ten backward to zero. With each count, see, feel, or imagine light entering through the top of your head.

Ten—the relaxation moves down through the crown of your head, opening up the skylight of your mind, allowing the sunlight to pour through, smoothing out any lines on your face, cleansing any worry away. The relaxation moves down through your eyes that are feeling so heavy now, as the muscles relax. You can try to open them, but it's so much easier to allow those totally relaxed muscles to just remain closed. The relaxation moves down further and further through your cheeks, jaw, and even your teeth.

Nine—this wonderful sensation makes its way down through your neck and shoulders, like a waterfall rushing down through your arms, massaging your shoulders, releasing any tension whatsoever.

Eight—it drifts down through your breathing area, as you take in another cleansing breath. This breath allows the relaxation to penetrate through your lungs and heart, which continues to beat without you needing to do a thing.

Seven—continue to feel the relaxation move down deeper and deeper into your stomach area, relaxing deep inside your back and stomach muscles.

Six—this sensation warms and relaxes you totally and completely. Like a sponge, you are soaking up the warmth and relaxation deep into your hips and pelvic area.

Five—relaxation is now flooding deeper down. With each exhalation you release a little more than you thought you could. This wonderful relaxation continues down through your thighs.

Four—imagine sunlight moving down through every atom, cell, and molecule of your being, as the relaxation moves deep down into your knees.

Three—the relaxation now moves down into your ankles.

Two—as it continues to move through your feet and through every single toe, you might notice your right foot beginning to tingle and then your left foot. Any last bit of tension blows out through the soles of your feet.

One—every ounce of your body is tingling with relaxation. Every cell is open, aware, and sparkling as your body prepares for deep and total relaxation.

Zero—deep asleep. Each and every time you hear or read "deep asleep," you go quickly, soundly, and deeply to this depth or deeper, for the purpose of surrendering to a deeply receptive state of self-hypnosis to assist you in improving your golf game. Surrender now as you go deep asleep.

Now you are entering that state of deep and total relaxation. You are here now at the level where your subconscious mind will do all the work for you, as your conscious mind drifts off. You are now in the place where all change takes place, easily, effortlessly. You are in total relaxation and total transformation. You are now at the center of your power. When you are in the Zone, all the cells in your body begin to transform and regenerate; new ideas and mental formations begin to align and take place. Now allow yourself to go deep asleep, deeper and deeper each time you read or hear this word.

You are now learning to relax tensions at the conscious level, so that your subconscious mind can assume its proper role in your golf swing. You will find that this alone produces the automatic, fluid swing that you want so very much. You are learning to use your subconscious mind to swing the stroke and hit the ball. Let your subconscious mind, the 88 percent of your mind's reasoning power, calculate which clubs to use and how to position yourself in the most advantageous way possible. This is the job it was designed to do, naturally, effortlessly, and efficiently.

Now take a few moments to see yourself out on your favorite golf course. It's a beautiful, sunny day. You feel the sun warming your shoulders and face. Smell the freshly cut, green grass, feel the briskness of the air, see the richness of this beautiful place that has been laid out before you. Take a deep breath, and breathe in the clean, fresh air. Notice and observe yourself taking a few swings. Watch the way you move, swing, and hit the ball. Time has slowed down, and you can actually observe yourself, movement by movement, in slow motion. Notice your momentum, your style, exactly as you are now, in your present state of expertise. Notice your strengths, and notice the areas that are challenging for you—from all angles, top, bottom, all sides.

Now, imagine, see, or sense that your favorite golf pro has just joined you. See what your golf pro looks like. Your pro has come out today specifically to assist you in becoming a better golfer. Watch him or her take a few swings. Watch, see, and feel the grace, the ease, the precision, and the fluidity of your pro's motion again, in slow motion. Notice every detail of his or her style and grace. From where you stand, you have X-ray vision that enables you to watch your pro from all angles: from top to bottom, and even to the inner workings of his or her muscles, joints, cells, and mind. As you continue to observe your favorite golf pro play at the height of his or her game, silently count from five backward to zero. As you do, with each deep breath you take, you are go to begin to merge with your golf pro.

Five—notice your heartbeats beginning to synchronize, beating in rhythm with each other.

Four—you are moving closer and closer to each other.

Three—the breathing of both of you is in sync.

Two—feel a profound sense of connection, power, clarity, and focus becoming amplified within you.

One—take one last breath to anchor and integrate into your body the change that has just taken place.

Zero—deep asleep. Each and every time you hear or read "deep asleep," you go quickly, soundly, and deeply to this depth or deeper, and your body relaxes. You and your golf pro are completely merged together as one. Take a few deep breaths and feel what it feels like to embody all of this skill and genius. Notice how different this feels and yet how familiar it is.

Now imagine that you begin to hit a bucket of balls as this golf pro. Place the ball on the tee. Choose your club. Now stand and position yourself, align your body, and you note the target you are aiming for. Look down at the ball and, as you take a deep, centering breath with eyes closed, silently say to yourself, "Zone in." This is your trigger to access your natural genius and focus completely on this moment.

All other thoughts except for hitting this ball leave your mind as you lift the club back and swing. Feel the wonderful rush of quiet, calm energy that floods your body as your ball soars through the air and lands in the exact spot you had intended for it. Notice the glances of admiration and respect from the other golfers around you.

Take a moment to savor this rich feeling. Allow your cells, atoms, and brain tissue to become saturated with the sensation of being in the Zone. You now realize that the more time you spend here, the deeper the groove in your subconscious mind becomes, and the stronger your anchor is here in the Zone. Now you will be able to access the Zone more readily, whenever you desire. Now see yourself hitting the rest of the balls in the bucket in exactly the same way.

Each and every time you do this, you are conditioning yourself to become a more skillful golfer. You are becoming like the sculpture of David, the masterpiece that Michelangelo freed from the marble. Each time you enter the Zone, more marble is chipped away; old ideas and habits that used to serve you in the past now cascade off of you.

Now that you are stronger, more comfortable, and more confident in your golf game than ever before, with these last few balls you have left in your bucket, try an experiment. Try to play like you used to play. You'll find the harder you try to play the old way, the more difficult it becomes, but just as an experiment, go ahead and give it a try. The more you try, the harder it becomes, because this new way of playing has already taken root deeply and profoundly in your subconscious mind. No matter how hard you try, this new way of playing will keep taking over.

Even in your sleep tonight, images and visions of you golfing at peak performance will keep cycling through your mind. In fact, don't be surprised if, for the rest of the day and even into tomorrow, the next day, and on into the future these images keep replaying through your mind. These images, like a movie that keeps looping over and over, become habit, a part of your cell tissue and your muscle memory. In fact, every time you hear the word *Zone*, waves of calm, peace, and a very joyful sensation rush through your entire body. Every time you think or hear *Zone*, a flush and rush of electricity runs through your body, and you can't help but feel great, confident, strong, and more powerful than ever before.

In a few moments, you will count from zero to five. At zero, you'll go deep asleep, deeper than ever before, and at five you'll be wide awake, alert, and aware, and feeling great.

Zero—deep asleep, deeper than ever before.

Acknowledge yourself for taking this time for yourself, for giving yourself the gift of taking control of your life, for doing something that will help you achieve more success not only in your golf game but also in all areas of your life.

Make an inner commitment to yourself to take the actions necessary to fulfill your intention to be the best golfer and person you can be. Nod your head right now, signaling to your subconscious mind that you are in agreement.

One—you feel physically relaxed and rejuvenated.

Two—notice feelings of emotional calm and peacefulness.

Three—with this breath, you are aware that something wonderful is about to happen to you.

Four—become aware of the air on your skin, and slightly move your fingers and toes to signal that you are about to awake, to have integrated in you all that you have just experienced, deep in your subconscious mind. Now, take a big deep breath as a feeling of well-being washes over you.

Five—open your eyes. You are wide awake, completely awake, and aware, and feeling great.

Secret Takeaways

- It is scientifically proven that music is one of the quickest ways to shift your state of mind and put you in the Zone.
- Because you are a unique human being, the music that alters your state of mind and puts you in the Zone is as one-of-a-kind as you are.

ZONE OUT

Win the game before you play

Everyone already has the resources they need to make the changes required to meet their goals.

—Milton H. Erickson

Secret Synopsis

Arrive at the golf course after already playing a winning game…in your mind. If you prepare, play by play, shot by shot, imagining in detail your ideal game, you are already on your way to a winning game of golf.

Plan Your Trip

Some successful golfers arrive at the golf course after already having played a winning game—in their minds. The exercise is simple but requires a degree of concentration, ideally done the morning before a game.

In your mind's eye, if you practice golfing in a state of perfection, that is what will make for a perfect game. In the theater of your mind, you are the director, actor, and writer of your movie. You can imagine your perfect grip, perfect swing stroke, perfect body alignment, perfect ability to know the distance to measure each putt, and perfect mental state. Practicing the art of perfecting your golf game, whether mentally or physically, creates an environment that supports an enhanced game.

Preparing for the Hall-of-Fame Self-Hypnosis Script

Although everyone's mental strategies for hitting golf balls are different, what is common to all of us is that we must be in an appropriate mood or emotional state of mind for a particular strategy to activate. When you are feeling dejected, you attract emotional sharks, as if you're bleeding in the water. On the golf course, when you start feeling discouraged, you attract more bad shots. You need an anchor to jolt you into a mood that unconsciously activates your best state.

Everyone has victorious moments in life—these can be triumphant moments when you were golfing or maybe a time you scored a touchdown or invited someone on a date or were recognized unexpectedly at work for a job well done.

When you intentionally recall a moment from your past when all was going your way and you were on top of your game, you draw from your personal hall of fame. Also, your breathing becomes deeper, your lungs fill to a fuller capacity, your posture straightens, your brain chemistry is altered, your confidence exudes, and you unconsciously begin to realign your frame of reference from a place that is patterned for more success.

Before you step foot on the golf course, perhaps at home the morning before your game or even in your car moments before you begin, you want to mentally visit your hall of fame and take a snapshot (the memory) of one of your greatest moments.

Warning

Your hall of fame exercise may seem counterintuitive to your inner critic. Keep in mind that it is the job of the inner critic to make sure that you don't at any time, ever, ever, look stupid. The notion of turning a deaf ear to the chiding and berating as you develop the new habit of tuning in only to the praise of your hall of fame may seem insane to the former you.

You might hear your inner critic say, "Listen All-High-and-Mighty, how else will you possibly improve if you just go around all day patting yourself on the back with that silly grin on your face. If you don't listen to me tell you what's wrong with you, you will make an ass out of yourself—and you're going to look so stupid that you will be a disgrace to your friends, colleagues, and family. In fact, you will be shunned and will never be asked back to play, which means social death, which is just a step away from actual death. In other words, if you don't listen to me, *you're gonna die!*"

Can you see the ridiculousness of the inner critic's logic? Are you really going to die from being happy on the golf course? In spite of its overprotective stranglehold, the inner critic actually doesn't need to be fired; it simply needs a job reassignment. As with a spinning top, when you operate at a higher level of energy, things no longer are black and white. See whether you can transfer your ego to a new task: letting you know when you are out of vibrational alignment with what it is that you truly want. Let your ego be the vibration police so that it can alert you when you've fallen off the Zone wagon and need to pay a visit to your hall of fame.

As time goes on, you will find many new moments of glory to add to your personal hall of fame.

Hall-of-Fame Self-Hypnosis Script

Your Zone Golf Hypnosis Journey

Sit in a comfortable, quiet position, or recline with your head slightly elevated.

Uncross your arms and legs, and rest your hands, palms up, either by your sides or on your thighs.

Should an emergency arise at any time while in self-hypnosis, you can get up to take care of the situation simply by counting yourself up from zero to five. At five you will be wide awake, completely alert, and aware.

Make sure you are in a comfortable position in a place where you will be uninterrupted for about 20 minutes.

Close your eyes and begin taking a few deep breaths. As you breathe, imagine a warm, comforting light entering through the crown of your head. Imagine a color that represents success to you, and begin counting down from ten to zero.

Ten—relax down through the crown of your head, opening up the door to your mind and allowing that wonderful color that represents success to intensify as it streams into your mind, filling your thoughts with this color that represents success and achievement to you.

Nine—the relaxation moves down and allows each breath to relax the thousands of muscles in your face. Envision the color that stimulates success within you, the color that relaxes you and at the same time inspires you.

Eight—relax and let go through your neck and shoulders and arms, feeling saturated with this vivid color of success.

Seven—the color of success and relaxation moves deeper down.

Six—notice this vibrant color drifting down through your breathing area. As you take in another cleansing breath, allow the relaxation to penetrate your lungs and heart. You are basking in that color of brilliant success.

Five—your relaxation is deepening down through your stomach, relaxing deep inside the muscles in your back and stomach, as you digest success on a deeper level than you ever have before.

Five—relaxation gently moves down through your pelvic area.

Four—totally and completely warmed and relaxed, you are being filled with the feeling tone of success.

Three—success is moving deeper down through your thighs. As the relaxation deepens with each breath, moving through your knees, the feeling and color of success intensify with each breath you take.

Two—this color that represents success is becoming brighter and brighter as you feel lighter and lighter, as it moves down into your feet.

One—success is tingling down in your toes now. Your body is flooded with the intense feeling and color of success.

Zero—deep asleep. Each and every time you read or hear "deep asleep," you go quickly, soundly, deeply to this depth or deeper, for the purpose of improving your golf game and enhancing your well-being. You are completely relaxed and receptive to the energy of success at the deepest level of your being.

Now trace through your history to a particular moment in the past that represents success to you. Take your time to remember. (Allow a few moments of silence.)

You may find many moments, or it might be a challenge to find a moment that appeals to you. Take your time until you resonate with a particular memory from your past when you felt the essence of success.

Become as specific as you can with one particular moment. As you take the next few deep breaths, try to distill this memory into a snapshot. Once you've crystallized the essence of the best moment, ponder the following questions with as much of your imagination and recall as possible:

- What was the time of day or night?
- What sounds did you hear around you?
- What was the temperature in the room?
- What were the colors around you?
- Were there other people present?
- Do you remember any scents?
- What was you inner dialogue?
- What did you tell yourself about yourself?
- Did you realize that you are more powerful than you realized, more capable and brilliant?
- Most important, how did you feel in your body (e.g., exalted, joyous, in love, powerful, special)?

Now magnify this feeling, making it as big as you can possibly imagine, as if this scene were playing on a gigantic movie screen, projected onto the sky. Allow it to fill your entire vision, engulfing the entire golf course and every blade of grass. Allow yourself to be imprinted with this exultation. Become aware of any distracting thoughts that might try to dampen this experience (the "don't get too happy" police). Explore how long you can contain this blissful experience. Try to contain it long enough for it to saturate and expand your sense of self, to expand who you think you are as a golfer and as a human being. Test yourself and imagine successfully embodying this new expanded exalted sense of self.

If you could distill this memory into a single word, what would it be? Would it be *love*, *victorious*, *powerful*, *passionate*, *abundant*, *triumphant*, or *alive*? Choose the word that most aptly describes you in this victorious moment. This is now your key word.

Take three deep breaths while saying this key word silently to yourself to lock in the feeling.

Now, imagine that you are on the golf course and you find yourself caught in a sand trap, having to make a bunker shot, a chip shot from deep grass to a close-cut pin, or making a breaking putt on a slick green. Choose the situation that would be the most difficult for you to make, the shot that would prompt your old familiar negative loop to start playing in your mind.

Call your hall-of-fame key word to mind. Breathe deeply three times, and allow yourself the luxury of ruminating in this feeling for at least 10–20 seconds, until you develop the habit of associating these difficult shots with a glorious feeling from your hall of fame.

When you are ready, see yourself now swinging the club and meeting this challenge with success. See that you are smiling, because you have now associated this challenging situation with success. Now go deep asleep. Each and every time you read "deep asleep" you go quickly, soundly, deeply to this depth or deeper. You are now completely relaxed and receptive to the energy of success on the deepest level of your being.

Now that you have learned how to meet golf's most challenging moments with great success this newfound skill will assist you not only in doing better in challenging moments but also in maintaining your sense of oneness and optimism even when things don't go according to plan.

Take three deep breaths as you prepare to come back.

Zero—go deep asleep, quickly, soundly, and deeply to this depth or deeper.

One—you feel tingly and begin to awaken, feeling the color of success saturating your inner vision.

Two—you feel emotionally calm, rested, and expanded. You are successful and connected to the oneness.

Three—notice a feeling of well-being washing your entire being, as the color of success encodes itself within you.

Four—become aware of a sense that something wonderful is about to happen to you. Look for it, prepare for it, and welcome it in when it shows up. Acknowledge yourself for all the great work you have been doing and for all that you continue to do.

Five—open your eyes. You are wide awake, alert, and aware, and you are feeling great.

Preparing for the Tower-of-Power Self-Hypnosis Script

This is your Tower-of-Power self-hypnosis script for immediate access to the Zone. This script is designed to illuminate all negative or limiting programming from the past to eliminate it, thereby giving you the key to being and becoming the best golfer you are capable of becoming.

Reading or listening to this script will restore your power, motivation, and commitment to play golf in the best way that you possibly can. Each time you listen to this program, you more readily absorb and memorize the information. Enjoy your self-hypnosis.

Tower-of-Power Self-Hypnosis Script

Your Zone Golf Hypnosis Journey

Sit in a comfortable, quiet position, or recline with your head slightly elevated.

Uncross your arms and legs, and rest your hands, palms up, either by your sides or on your thighs.

Should an emergency arise at any time while in self-hypnosis, you can get up to take care of the situation simply by counting yourself up from zero to five. At five you will be wide awake, completely alert, and aware.

Sit in a comfortable position in a room or a place where you will be uninterrupted for about 20 minutes.

Close your eyes. Place your thumb and forefinger together on your right hand.

Begin by taking some deep breaths. Fill up with air that you hold for a count of five.

One, two, three. Four—press your thumb and forefinger together. Five—let go of the breath and release the thumb and forefinger.

Your mind and body, your subconscious, will remember this signal. Begin to count backward from ten to zero. Once you arrive at zero you will go deep asleep, and enter a deep, restful state in which you are extremely suggestible and open to the positive suggestions you are about to receive.

And now begin counting from ten down to zero. Imagine you have entered an elevator that has ten floors. You begin at the tenth floor, and with each descending floor, you go rapidly into a deeper, more comfortable level of hypnosis.

Watch as the light in the elevator illuminates the tenth floor. As you drop down to the ninth floor, you find your body relaxing and letting go.

You move down to the eighth floor, noticing that with each descending number, you are letting yourself enjoy a deepening comfort and are letting go of all stress.

Dropping down to the seventh floor you allow yourself to drop into that place of deep ease.

You are drifting and dropping deeper down to the sixth floor, and you perhaps feel more relaxed than you have ever been in your entire life.

You are descending to the fifth floor comfortably, rapidly, and easily. You continue down to the fourth and then the third floor, as you drop more deeply as you come to the second floor.

As you take this next deep breath, you find yourself all the way down at the first floor, yet you continue down to zero. You are now in the basement, and you go deep asleep. Each and every time you read or hear "deep asleep," you go quickly, soundly, and deeply to this depth or deeper, for the purpose of preparing to be the best golfer you are capable of being.

You are entering a very special, private place in yourself as you continue all the way down into a wonderful, comfortably relaxed sensation of being balanced and at the center of yourself.

Ignite your imagination by seeing that you are standing in front of an ornate, red door. On the door is a sign that says, "Your greatest golf potential." You feel a sensation of curiosity and excitement rise up in you, a desire to open that door and see what is behind it. You try to open it but can't because it is locked. For a moment, you sense a feeling of disappointment, until you reach into your pocket to discover that you hold the key that unlocks this door to your greatest golf potential.

With excitement, you place the key in the lock and discover that the key fits perfectly. You turn the handle now, and this large, strong door now is open to you, and you feel that something wonderful is about to be revealed to you. You take a deep breath as you walk through the door and discover a beautiful stairwell spiraling upward with plush-carpeted steps.

With enthusiasm and a sense of adventure, you climb the stairs. You hold on to the handrail with your left hand and begin with your left foot, taking the steps, climbing higher and higher. As you climb this spiral staircase, you realize that you are ascending a tower.

See in your mind's eye or feel that you have climbed one hundred floors, but because you are in such great shape, you are barely winded. With the next deep breath, you reach the top of this spiral staircase and immediately discover another large red door. You already know that your key will open the door, and you are pleased when it does.

Once inside the door, you enter a circular tower that is somehow familiar to you. You look and see a table with the chalice of empowerment resting on it. There are windows around the circular wall. You look out the windows and see the tops of clouds below you. Above the clouds there is a bright blue sky and powerful sunlight that gives you a great sense of freedom and relief from the stress of the world below.

In the center of this room is a chair and mirror. There are skylights above you on this domed ceiling. You are in your tower of power. Everything in this room connects you with your most empowered self. In this room you have full access to the genius golfer that you are capable of becoming.

See yourself walking to the table. Lift the chalice of empowerment and drink from it. Even with only one swallow, you immediately begin to feel a tingling sensation, your spine lengthens, you feel taller, your body is more aligned, your breathing is deeper, and your thinking is clearer. Your nerves are relaxed and you feel restored.

From this moment forward, each and every time you take a drink of water when you are on the golf course, you will remember this feeling and you will associate water with empowerment. Take another drink, and repeat the experience (the tingling sensation, your spine lengthening, feeling taller, your body more aligned, breathing more deeply, and thinking more clearly). Your nerves are relaxed, and you feel restored. Deep asleep: quickly, soundly, and deeply to this depth or deeper.

Absorb the new anchor you just received. Each and every drink of water you have on the golf course creates a tingling sensation within you;

your spine lengthens; you feel taller and more aligned; you breathe more deeply and think more clearly, as you become relaxed and restored.

You move now to your chair that faces your mirror of wisdom and sit down. Feel yourself relax even more deeply as you melt into the softness of the plush cushions of the chair. Sitting in the chair, you feel a wave of complete comfort overcome you; all burdens and stress are now lifted from you. You are at peace, and you know that all the powerful resources you need to be your very best are now within you. In this chair, you relax more deeply because you are resting in your innate wisdom, and you go into a deeper level of relaxation than ever before.

Deep asleep. Each and every time you read or hear "deep asleep," you go quickly, soundly, deeply to this depth or deeper—and you become more and more receptive to the positive messages that assist you in becoming the greatest golfer you can possibly be.

Directly in front of you is the mirror of wisdom. In the mirror, you see the perfect image of yourself as the ideal golfer that you aspire to be, a true master of being in the Zone. Study the way your body looks and feels. In the mirror, you are now shown in slow motion the way you, as master golfer, grip and swing the clubs.

Notice from all angles the way your master golfer measures each putt, each stroke, each movement, and even chooses each club. Notice the grace, and the ease, the prowess, and the power of your master golfer.

Now notice this image is smiling lovingly at you and begins to speak to you: "I am so very proud of you. Your natural talent as a golfer is perfect as is your timing. I have been here within you all along, and you are now ready for what I have to show you."

Hearing these words you feel a deep inner peace and relief.

Your master golfer tells you, "There are no mistakes. Only unwanted results. You learn from them. It is simple. You can always have the results that you want by taking the action that brings about those results."

You feel encouraged and inspired as you listen on: "I am very happy that you have chosen to give yourself this empowerment. You deserve it. You are ready for this. I am very happy and proud of you."

Your master golfer motions with a graceful hand, "Come in and join me here, and feel what it feels like to step fully into your power as the master golfer that you truly are."

You stand up from this comfortable chair and step right into the mirror. You step right into the image of your master golfer—your most confident, empowered, genius self, and a true master of the game of golf.

Now take a few deep breaths as you absorb this transformation. Notice the difference in how you feel when you are inside the mirror, standing in the shoes of your master golfer.

Once you become acclimated here, allow a word to come to mind that describes this sensation (e.g., *power, clarity, grace, joy, satisfaction, control, success, awake*). Once you have chosen your word (it now becomes your key word), place your thumb and forefinger together on your right hand, give them a slight squeeze, and repeat your key word three times silently to yourself as you take three deep breaths. (Allow a few moments for this experience.)

As you do this, you are anchoring your connection to the master golfer that you naturally are. See yourself accessing this trigger on the golf course when about to tee off, and throughout your game any time you feel the need to reconnect with your master golfer. See yourself doing this now. (Allow a few moments for this experience, as much time as you need.)

The more often you access this anchor or revisit this program, you will enhance and deepen your ease of entry to the Zone and your identity as this master golfer within. Now go deep asleep, quickly, soundly, and deeply to this depth or deeper. Release your thumb and forefinger as you allow yourself to be flooded with well-being.

You realize that each and every time you touch your forefinger to your thumb, you have created an anchor that gives you access to visit your tower of power as well as your master golfer. When you access your tower of power, you immediately quench your thirst from the chalice of empowerment and feel the rush of focused awareness and peace of mind.

When you are in your tower of power, your negative self-talk and old limiting golf habits are removed and eliminated and your level of skill as a master golfer is exalted.

You step out of the mirror now, allowing the image of your master golfer to remain in the mirror. Now that you have stepped out of the mirror, look back into the mirror at the master golfer, at yourself. Examine yourself closely because you have changed. Scan your body to identify the ways in which your physical appearance is now more in accord than ever with your inner master golfer (you might look lighter, taller, slimmer, younger, more physically toned, more graceful, or more powerful; you might be smiling more radiantly). Feel that you now embody this change as you prepare to leave your tower of power.

Before you leave, the master golfer in the mirror says, "I have one last gift to share with you. Close your eyes and get ready for a powerful experience. It will become very bright so keep your eyes closed."

Your eyes are closed, and the skylight of your tower of power opens up and sunlight of awareness showers you with energy now. As this happens, though your eyes are closed, you can sense the intense brightness as the skylight above you allows a beam of powerful light to slowly descend on you. You feel the energy of the light spiraling through your body. You intuitively sense that this is a loving energy that lifts you up to an even higher level than ever before.

You hear or sense your master golfer say to you, "The old negative self-talk that used to run the show for you on the golf course as well as all your old limiting golf habits that used to define the way that you played in the past are now only shadows. And these shadows cannot hide from this sunlight of awareness."

Like shadows, the old limited and negative ways of being immediately disappear when the light is shown on them. Watch them dissolve in an instant back into the nothingness from which they came.

Take a deep breath, feeling the relief that comes from having your shadows dissolved, as you feel the light beam and sense its radiance. Your body absorbs the power of the sunlight of awareness, and you feel eager and excited to take this light that you now embody to the golf course.

Feel or see yourself in your mind's eye now, out on the golf course. You are smiling; feeling graceful but powerful as you swing, putt, and accurately measure the distance between each shot; and enjoying your game more than you ever have.

You are preparing to leave your tower of power now, and you realize that you can return any time you'd like because this is your special place. Make a pact to return here often, especially when you would like to feel rejuvenated and reminded of the master golfer you truly are.

Remember the key is in your hand. Walk back toward the door, down the spiral staircase, through the door, and step back into the elevator.

As you rise up each of the ten floors, starting with zero, you will feel an increased motivation and commitment to become the best golfer you can be.

One—the first floor. You feel grateful that you went on this journey up to the top of your tower of power.

Two—you notice a feeling of peacefulness and calm.

Three—you are feeling a powerful clarity and sense of integration and exhilaration.

Four—you sense that the energy of your tower of power is now encoded within you.

Five—you are becoming more and more awake.

Six—you are now moving higher and higher, preparing your body to be fully awake.

Seven—take some deep breaths.

Eight—recognize that something wonderful is happening to you.

Nine—you are becoming aware and are feeling refreshed and at ease.

Ten—you are now wide awake, completely alert, and aware, as your body awakens with a wonderful feeling of refreshment. When you are ready, open your eyes and take this empowerment with you to your golf game.

Thrive

Where attention goes, energy flows and results show.

If you truly want to improve your golf game, begin paying attention to what you are doing right. Has a boss ever criticized you for not doing the job according to his or her ideal? Did you feel motivated to do a better job or weakened by the comment? Was it more difficult to do the job you were doing? Conversely, have you ever been sincerely praised for doing a great job and felt the motivation to do an even better job? Why would it be any different on the golf course? In any given game, there are hundreds of things you are doing right. As you begin to be attuned to what those things are, you will notice an amplification of your ability to do even better.

Imagine that your talent, your natural genius, is like the most precious gold in the world. Just as in a museum, where precious objects are protected with guards and electrical alarms to ensure that they don't fall into the wrong hands, your genius is kept under lock and key. Consider that you are like the thief of your own treasure. Your job is to get past your own protective mechanisms to be able to access the gold within you. When you sincerely praise yourself for all that has gone right during your golf game, instead of berating yourself for all the little things you could have done better, you weaken the resistance of the guards and the electric fences that keep you from reaching your gold.

Up until now, your inner guards have had an important purpose. Our ability to strategically protect ourselves, both physically and emotionally, is a key to our survival.

However, I would wager that if all you were interested in was survival, you would not be reading this book or wanting to improve your golf game. I think you are no longer playing the survive game but instead the thrive game. And to do that, you must send your guards on a permanent coffee break.

Each and every time you hear the voice of your inner critic, realize that you are back in the old, Neanderthal survival paradigm and take a breath. As you breathe, you are buying yourself some time to make the choice to take contrary action.

Ordinary action would have you listen to your inner critic as if your critic were on the five o'clock news and reporting the truth. With contrary action, you would immediately hit the mute button, sidestep the television, and walk across the bridge to the land of thriving.

The Thrive Formula

Here is a six-step formula I created to help you remember how to cross the bridge from surviving to thriving:

1. Thankful
2. Heart centered
3. Release
4. Inspirational song
5. Visualize
6. Express

Once you've crossed the bridge from the land of surviving to the land of thriving, you will have some questions. In the land of surviving, there were no questions. Everything was laid out for you in a predictable fashion (e.g., do whatever you need to do not to look stupid, make as few embarrassing mistakes as possible, and play to win). However, in the land of thriving, the territory is not so well defined. There is no science to it because the sky is the limit of what you are capable of there. In the land of thriving, you are in uncharted territory because you live your own life, do not follow the code that your ancestors have set for you, and follow the dictates of your own soul.

Living in the land of thriving means you have upped the ante—you are moving from a good life to a great life, from being a mediocre golfer to a great golfer, from predictability to mystery.

You can look at survival as a science, but thriving is an art. Survival tells you that as a golfer, you are your past. Thriving tells you that you are a future that has not yet been defined. Thriving tells you that you have a destiny to be great.

Resources or Resourcefulness?

You might be reading this and thinking, "Well, if I had the money Tiger Woods has, it would be easy to thrive as a golfer," or "If I had the time that Lorena Ochoa has, then I would be better!" or "If I had the technology that is available to Jack Nicklaus, then I could be a better golfer."

Most people who lay claim to the land of survival blame their mediocre game on their limited resources—money, time, and/or technology. But those are not the defining factors of greatness. The defining factor is not resources but resourcefulness. Many of the great golfers you admire were not born with a silver golf club but made the best of what they were given to lay claim to the land of thriving.

A case in point is Angel Cabrera, winner of the 2007 U.S. Open golf championship, who is an icon of triumph against the odds. Cabrera was so poor that he could not afford shoes. His shoelessness revealed his big feet, and that was how he earned his nickname "El Pato" (the duck). He can attribute his extraordinary success not to a silver spoon but to his determination.

Preparing for the Thrive Self-Hypnosis Script

Before you read or listen to the Thrive self-hypnosis script, it will be helpful for you to begin with a brief understanding of what each section stands for.

With regard to "thankful," you will be asked to make a quick gratitude list, as gratitude is one of the quickest shifters of energy to assist in getting from surviving to thriving. By practicing this, you will become an expert at doing this on a dime. Here is an exercise to build your gratitude muscles. In the next 30 seconds, challenge yourself to make a written list of five things you are grateful for right now (e.g., having been out on the golf course today, feeling healthy enough to golf, having scored a birdie on your last shot, having found your new grip helpful in directing the ball to where you want it to go). (For more information on gratitude, see Secret #8.)

For "heart centered," you take three heart-centered breaths to help you shift your focus from your head to your heart, which is a shortcut to the Zone and the land of thriving. (For more information on heart-centered breathing, see Secret #3.)

R stands for "release." Release and let go of stress, overthinking, and trying to get it right. (For more information on releasing the mind, see Secret #2).

For "inspirational song," find a thrive song to add to your Zone Golf soundtrack that pumps you up and pulls you out of surviving into thriving. Some examples are "I Get Knocked Down," by Chumbawumba; "Centerfield," by John Fogerty; "New York, New York," by Frank Sinatra; or the theme song to *Chariots of Fire*, by Vangelis.

There is nothing like an inspirational song to grease the wheels of your ability to shift from zero to hero, from surviving to thriving. If you choose, you can cue it up to play during your self-hypnosis session. (For more information on the advantages of music in getting you in the Zone and keeping your there, see Secret #5).

For "visualize," envision your master golfer self and feel it move into you. Act as if you were this master golfer version of yourself. How does this golfer walk, talk, putt, swing, and so on? (For more information on your master golfer, see the Tower-of-Power self-hypnosis script).

For "expressive," express yourself through an action that shocks you because it is not ordinary. For example, throw your head back and yell, "Yes!" or clap your hands together three times and say your key word silently to yourself. By expressing a physical anchor that shocks your ordinary physicality, you will quickly jump from a surviving state to a thriving state. Identify what your action will be.

Thrive Self-Hypnosis Script

Your Zone Golf Hypnosis Journey

Sit in a comfortable, quiet position, or recline with your head slightly elevated.

Uncross your arms and legs, and rest your hands, palms up, either by your sides or on your thighs.

Should an emergency arise at any time while in self-hypnosis, you can get up to take care of the situation simply by counting yourself up from zero to five. At five you will be wide awake, completely alert, and aware.

Close your eyes and nod your head slightly, signaling to your subconscious mind that you are ready to enter a deep state of self-hypnosis to radically improve your golf game.

As you begin, take a few very deep breaths, and you may begin to notice certain parts of your body relaxing. Perhaps other parts are still a little tense. Just become aware of this, as your body continues to relax—the way your clothes feel on your body, the way the air feels as it gently brushes up against your face.

Notice your body being completely supported by the weight of the chair, couch, bed, or whatever it is that is holding you up.

As you read this, become aware of how good it feels to breathe in deeply and slowly, and to release completely. Feel your chest and stomach rise with each inhalation, and contract with each exhalation. Notice the release and the letting go that takes place now. With each breath that you exhale, you release all your cares of the day.

With each breath you breathe out, you let go of any and all tension that may linger in your body. And with each and every inhalation, you breathe in a sense of peace and relaxation.

Begin to count yourself down into a deeper state of relaxation. Start with five and move down to zero. At zero you will go deep asleep, a receptive state of focused relaxation. And with each count, you become more and more relaxed, and completely peaceful.

Begin with five, as you let go with each breath.

Four—all tension washes away.

Three—allow yourself to feel heavy in the chair or on whatever surface holds you up.

Two—let go more than before, as you prepare yourself to discover an inner resourcefulness that will improve the way you approach your golf game and relate to yourself as a golfer.

One—prepare to enter the Zone.

Zero—deep asleep. Each and every time you read or hear "deep asleep," you go quickly, soundly, and deeply to this depth or deeper for the purpose of entering the Zone and radically transforming your mental golf game.

Begin now to see yourself on the golf course that you will soon be playing. And imagine feeling very comfortable, relaxed, at ease, and in the Zone. Create an anchor in the land of thriving, starting with *T*, for "thankful." Call to mind five things for which you are thankful. (Allow a few moments to contemplate this.)

Allow thankfulness and gratitude to well up in you, becoming a stronger and stronger reference point for you with each breath. Inhale deeply and soak up the feeling and the attitude of gratitude, knowing that this simple action takes you from surviving consciousness to thriving consciousness. (Allow a few moments to linger in this feeling tone.)

Take another deep breath. Go deep asleep, quickly, soundly, and deeply to this depth or deeper.

And now move to heart-centered breathing. Take three deep breaths in, focusing your attention with each breath on the area around your heart. With each breath, imagine that the area around your heart begins to soften, to loosen up, and that all barriers begin to dissolve. Continue to focus your attention as you breathe into the area around your heart until you notice your heartbeat. It is beginning to become a gentler rhythm than before. Notice your heart rate becoming steady and coherent, smooth and even. Continue to hear and feel your heart beat beneath your chest, and relax more and more with each and every breath you take. (Allow a few moments to linger in this feeling tone.)

Take another deep breath, and go deep asleep, quickly, soundly, and deeply to this depth or deeper.

And now release. Imagine that you are standing under a waterfall or a rain shower, and all stress and strain is washing from you and down the drain. Continue to breathe as you focus on letting go of all ties to the land of surviving. You are now allowing yourself to feel refreshed, reborn. Now that you have a clear slate from which to begin anew, let your next three breaths revive and renew you, delivering you, as if for the first time, to the land of thriving. (Allow a few moments to linger in this feeling tone.)

Take another deep breath. Go deep asleep, quickly, soundly, and deeply to this depth or deeper.

Now move to your inspirational song. If you already have your "thrive" song or Zone Golf soundtrack on your MP3 player, take a few minutes to play that song now. If you don't have it on your MP3 player, then take a moment to imagine the song and hear it play in your mind. Allow yourself to imagine the music, the rhythm, and the lyrics. Move your way to the part of the song that most inspires you. Turn up the volume of the song, even blast it, elevating you higher and higher, pumping you up and pulling you out of surviving into a magnificent state of thriving. (Allow a few moments to linger in this song and the feeling tone it produces.)

Take another deep breath, and go to deep asleep, quickly, soundly, and deeply to this depth or deeper.

And now visualize your inner master golfer. How does this genius version of you walk, talk, putt, swing? What do you look like, feel like, sound like, and golf like when you are fully thriving? Allow an image of this version of yourself to imprint your mind and inspire your action. (Allow a few moments to linger in this feeling tone of your master golfer.)

Take a deep breath, and go deep asleep, quickly, soundly, and deeply to this depth or deeper.

Express yourself. Envision your physical action, the one that you chose to shock you into thriving. Visualize it, and express it.

Feel the exhilaration of this action and notice how your state changes. Feel the difference between where you were and where you are now. (Allow a few moments to linger in this feeling tone.)

Take a deep breath, and go deep asleep, quickly, soundly, and deeply to this depth or deeper.

Envision yourself having a survival moment on the green (e.g., you shanked the ball, overshot your putt, or are nervous because you are about to play with strangers or people you want to impress). As soon as your old berating inner critic begins to have its way with you, your thrive formula automatically kicks in:

You become thankful, giving thanks for five things you are grateful for.

You become heart centered, taking three breaths in and around your heart.

You release, allowing your breathing to help you become a whole new you.

You play your inspirational song in your mind, connecting you with the feeling and the sound of thriving.

You visualize your master golfer self and feel it move into you and inform the way you walk, talk, putt, swing, think, and feel.

You express your physical anchor that shocks you out of surviving right into thriving.

Anchor in thriving with one more deep breath, knowing that these things will go with you wherever you go. Especially when you detect that you have stepped into a survival land mine, thriving will kick in automatically, habitually, quickly, to help you become the best golfer you can possibly be. And now go deep asleep, quickly, soundly, and deeply to this depth or deeper.

See that now you are adept in the land of thriving, and this is your new set point. In fact, as hard as you might try to go back across the bridge to the land of survival, it is impossible. But go ahead and try to do that now. The harder you try, the more difficult it becomes, because your new set point is in thriving. Let it go now as you go deep asleep.

You are now reveling in thriving. It is becoming habitual to give thanks, to breathe in a heart-centered way, to release negativity, to be inspired, to visualize your master golfer, and to express yourself when you need to catapult yourself from surviving to thriving.

Very good. Take another deep breath as you prepare yourself to move upward from zero to five.

Zero—go deep asleep, quickly, soundly, and deeply to this depth or deeper.

One—you feel tingly and begin to awaken.

Two—you feel emotionally calm, rested, and expanded, and you begin to feel the integration of all that you experienced.

Three—a feeling of well-being floods your entire body, and you are becoming completely integrated and organized in the consciousness of thriving.

Four—you feel a sensation of gratitude welling up in you for yourself, for your willingness to thrive.

Five—know that changes have already begun in your golf game and in your life. With excitement, allow your eyes to open as you become wide awake, alert, and aware. You are feeling great and fully alive—you are thriving!

Secret Takeaways

- There are no mistakes, only unwanted results.
- The practice of perfection makes perfect.
- Exaggerate your memories from your hall of fame to ten times their intensity to associate them more deeply with your golf game.
- You are the thief of your very own golfer's gold.
- You can look at survival as a science and thriving as an art.

SLEEP YOUR WAY TO SUCCESS

Find the ZZZs in the Zone

What other people may find in poetry or art museums, I find in the flight of a good drive—the white ball sailing up into the blue sky, growing smaller and smaller, then suddenly reaching its apex, curving, falling and finally dropping to the turf to roll some more, just the way I planned it.

—Arnold Palmer

Secret Synopsis

Every person, without exception, can transform any fragility to fortune, tragedy to triumph, and a weak golf score to one that will make him or her stand and cheer. Maximizing the accessibility of your subconscious mind in the moments before and during sleep is one of the fastest ways to improve your golf game and your life. Secret #7 is about integrating dreamwork, affirmations, and the law of attraction. This is the magic formula to bring about quantum change on and off the golf course.

Dreams

Are our dreams—that wild, fantastic, and uncensored jumble of images that bombard our sleep—just a recapitulation of our day's events, or are they more? Can you open your mind to the possibility that your dreams might actually bear gifts, valuable gifts to help you gain guidance, solve problems, and figure out your magic formula for straightening out your swing?

I believe the answer to that question is an unequivocal yes. It has been my experience as a hypnotherapist and spiritual coach that dreams provide a valuable mental resource for helping people to understand the inner urgings that are trying to help them grow and improve in the areas that are important to them. I have found that dreams, my own and those of my clients, contain messages—messages from our subconscious to our conscious. In addition, when we begin to consciously work with our dreams, we receive insights throughout the day that can help us connect with a greater level of guidance, intuition, and wisdom.

As Robert Van de Castle writes in his book *Our Dreaming Mind*, golf legend Jack Nicklaus told a *San Francisco Chronicle* reporter that he attributed his success in part to a dream he had years ago: "Wednesday night I had a dream and it was about my golf swing. I was hitting them pretty good in the dream and all at once I realized I wasn't holding the club the way I've actually been holding it lately. I've been having trouble collapsing my right arm, taking the club head away from the ball, but I was doing it perfectly in my sleep. So when I came to the course yesterday morning I tried it the way I did in my dream and it worked. I shot a sixty-eight yesterday and a sixty-five today."

Using the brain's natural alpha state—the time just before sleep—you will learn how to redraw the subconscious mind's unhealthy picture of you as a golfer and create one that reflects the best golfer you can possibly be.

When you are asleep, you are in the most vulnerable, suggestible state of being. This is magic time, when the 88 percent of your mind's power is truly accessible. The guards at the gate (e.g., your inner critic) are asleep, leaving access to your most valuable asset: your subconscious mind. Maximizing the accessibility of your subconscious mind in the moments before and during sleep and on awakening is one of the fastest ways to passively affect your golf game. If you saturate your subconscious mind with thoughts that imprint you golfing moment by moment in your ultimate state, it will be impossible to not see an improvement the next day on the course.

As a hypnotherapist and dream expert, I feel a strong pull toward the traditions that teach that the dream world may be more real, not less real, than the world of our conscious reality. Perhaps our greatest wisdom and our best golf guidance (and who knows, maybe even the winning lottery numbers) are to be found in dream time.

Our dream time does not occur only while we sleep. In fact, we weave in and out of our dream time throughout the day. Every time you hear a song that tugs on those nostalgic heartstrings, your mind reels back in time to a special moment you associate with the song. These are day-to-day moments of falling down the rabbit hole into a deeper state of feeling and sense memory.

When we enter a state of hypnosis, we slip through the cracks of the waking world of our five senses, where our desires and limitations run the show, and we connect to the world of the soul. The soul is akin to the world we enter when we are asleep, where our consciousness is expanded and we fly free and explore our unlimited possibilities. Hypnosis is the bridge between those worlds.

If it is true that we only use 12 percent of our mind's power, leaving 88 percent untapped, then it is as if we were sleeping on a gold mine. Yet when we awaken, we live our lives as if we were impoverished beings, limping along the golf course, complaining about the same score as always. But what would happen to your life (much less your golf game) if you were to suddenly explore and master the dormant 88 percent of your mind's power?

Secret #7 may be the easiest and most forward-moving, results-oriented section of the entire Zone Golf program. You can do most of the work lying down! If you read or listen to the self-hypnosis scripts that accompany this section before drifting off to sleep in the evenings before a golf game, you will quicken the improvement of your golf game and condition your mind with very positive messages of health and well-being.

Sleep Your Way to Success

To maximize your dream time, you want to situate yourself in the most beneficial way possible, bringing into your dream time a relic from your hypnosis journey. You also want to ensure that you maximize your dream and sleep time in the most opportune way with the following simple checklist:

Sight

DO	DON'T
DO make sure your bedroom looks tidy and orderly.	DON'T allow your room to be cluttered with debris, and close your closet and drawers.
DO make sure that the pictures on the wall or that you see before drifting off to sleep are uplifting ones (e.g., a picture of you striking a powerful golf pose or your favorite professional golfer).	DON'T hang photos or pictures that are negative or frightening.
DO watch movies or TV programs that are life affirming.	DON'T fall asleep watching the news or movies about disaster.

Sound

DO	DON'T
DO allow white noise, such as a fan or air purifier, to block out jarring or distracting sounds.	DON'T fall asleep with the television on (the abrupt sounds such as slamming doors or sirens will disrupt you from having the deepest sleep possible).
DO listen to the Secret #7 audio track, Hot Air Balloon (track 3 on the accompanying CD), to help you sleep deeply and to positively program your subconscious mind with images and sensations of you golfing at your peak potential.	DON'T listen to any news or any audio program that is discouraging or not uplifting.
DO get an alarm that can wake you gradually in the morning (e.g., an MP3 player, or a Zen Alarm Clock that wakes you with a gradually increasing series of Tibetan bell–like chimes.	

Smell

DO	DON'T
DO make sure that there is a pleasant scent in your room as you sleep.	DON'T allow dead flowers or an opened bathroom door to allow unpleasant smells in the bedroom.
DO use scented fabric softeners on your sheets and pillowcases.	DON'T use perfumes or fabric softeners that cause an allergic reaction.

Touch

DO	DON'T
DO make sure that your sheets and bedding feel pleasant, soft, fuzzy, or silky on your skin.	DON'T sleep with pillows or sheets that feel scratchy or unpleasant.
DO place a pen and paper by your bedside to take note of any dreams you recall as soon as you awaken in the morning.	DON'T let the room get too hot or too cold.

Taste

DO	DON'T
DO brush your teeth before bedtime to keep your breath as fresh as possible as you sleep, especially after a midnight snack that includes strong flavors, such as garlic or fruit juice. Unpleasant scents and tastes have been scientifically proven to have an adverse affect on your sleep and dreams.	DON'T go to bed with your taste buds drenched in garlic, tobacco, or other strong flavors.
DO have a glass of water by your bedside to quench your thirst in the middle of the night.	DON'T drink fruit juice in the middle of the night; the sugar creates an unpleasant aftertaste.

Zone Golf Affirmation—Seeds to Plant in the Garden of Your Dreams

Where is your mind focused right now?

Our minds go wherever we aim them. Personal growth seminar leader T. Harv Eker says, "Where attention goes, energy flows, and results show." In other words, you will get more of whatever you focus on. For example, if you focus on screwing up your next shot, then your shot will go everywhere but straight. However, if you focus on feeling good and you rhythmically swing your club in the right direction, you will get that result.

Most of us are distracted by all things bright and shiny. We let our minds go to whatever pops up and grabs our attention. We don't exert the mind mastery that is ours to control. So how do you escape this mental sand trap?

Affirmations

An affirmation is a positive statement that you repeat over and over and again to condition your mind to think in a way that resonates with the outcomes you wish to create in your life. Think of it like this: your ears hear what your mouth says. Your words are the tools with which you craft your life. Affirmations can be written down, spoken aloud, or read silently. When affirmations are brief, worded positively, and emotionally charged with vivid images attached to them, they become mental magnets that draw to you the people, places, and situations that align with your greatest desires.

Affirmations that are concise, clear, and deeply felt are better than ones that are vague, verbose, and superficial. Consider the following great affirmations:

"I am the golfer I choose to be."

"Every day in every way, my golf game is getting better."

"I am my personal best, and I am proud of myself."

"I am improving my golf swing every time I play."

"I trust my instincts to choose the right club."

"I have the balance of strength and control when I am putting."

"I hit the ball straight and long."

"No matter what, I enjoy myself every time I play."

Key Points to Consider When Crafting Your Zone Golf Affirmations

These are the simple steps to creating effective golf affirmations, which align your conscious mind with your subconscious mind and help you actualize your dreams of becoming a Zone golfer.

Keep It Positive

Think about your ideal golf scene and allow your affirmations to describe the scene in the most positive way possible. Affirm what you do want, not what you don't want. For example, "I am no longer slicing the ball" is a negative statement. Instead, affirm, "I am hitting the ball directly where I want it to go." This statement is much more powerful because it is positive, reinforces your desired goal, and doesn't confuse your subconscious mind with the mention of the undesirable condition.

Make It Elegant and to the Point

When you create your affirmation briefly and to the point it has the most punch. Concise affirmations not only are easiest to remember but also have far greater subconscious magnetism than those that are long and wordy.

Speak It in the Here and Now

A powerful affirmation is written or expressed in the moment. For example, "I hit the ball with a penetrating trajectory." Affirming something in the future tense, like "I am going to hit the ball with a penetrating trajectory," programs it to always be just beyond your reach.

Make It Yours

Think about the words that are personally meaningful to you. Craft your affirmations with words and phrases that light you up and inspire on. The more passion you can pack into your affirmation, the more powerful the results will be.

Stretch Yourself

Your affirmation should stretch you toward an outcome that you have yet to accomplish but not too far outside what you can conceive of. For example, if your current handicap is 19 and you want it to be 9, that is definitely in the realm of possibility. Belief will grow as you begin to experience success with this process.

Feel It First

Spend a few moments every day feeling and imagining what it will be like when you fulfill the desire that you're affirming. In other words, feel with every fiber of your being that your desire has happened. As you do this, you are becoming a master at the law of attraction, which puts you in resonance with that which you seek.

Unleash Your Passion

Give yourself permission to feel the excitement, the joy, the relief, and the exaltation of having your ideal scene realized.

The Law of Attraction

The law of attraction is that like attracts like. This is believed to be a powerful universal law, and it is key to manifesting the life and the results that you desire.

What Is a Universal Law?

Universal laws govern our world and apply to the basic principles of life that have been around since creation. Take gravity, for example, and the laws of aerodynamics. These universal laws are not personal in that they apply to everyone, everywhere, and they cannot be broken or changed.

The law of attraction is another such universal law, and the law of attraction has everything to do with the mental game of golf. More than in any other sport, golfers have the best opportunity to truly hone their law-of-attraction skills, because so much of the game takes place between their ears. Learning to become a master of the law of attraction will not only improve your golf game but also raise your level of enjoyment of the game to a whole new level.

The law of attraction is working in your life right now, whether or not you are aware of it. You attract the people, situations, jobs, and golf score that you are in resonance with. Once you are aware of the law of attraction and how it works, you can start to use it to deliberately attract what you want into your life, in your golf game, and beyond.

If this seems like a foreign concept, consider that you may be familiar with these other ways of expressing it:

- Birds of a feather flock together.
- You are a magnet for what you think about.
- What you are looking for, you are looking with.
- "As a man thinks in his heart, so is he" (Proverbs 23:7).
- You reap what you sow.

The Secret behind the Secret

Most people have seen or at least heard about the vastly popular movie and best-selling book *The Secret*. Created by Rhonda Byrne and inspired by the work of Esther and Jerry Hicks, *The Secret* reveals that the knowledge of the law of attraction has been the basis of all great things that have been accomplished throughout history.

The secret behind the secret is that if you are not getting the life circumstances or golf score you want, then you are not a vibrational match to those circumstances. This is the bad news and the good news. The bad news is that you are not a vibrational match to the results you desire (ouch!). However, the good news is that changing your vibration is completely under your control.

When you read the self-hypnosis scripts in this section before going to sleep, you will be creating a new vibrational set point for yourself and thus closing the gap between where you are and where you want to be.

Preparing for the Hot-Air-Balloon Self-Hypnosis Script

The following self-hypnosis script has been designed to assist you in taking your mastery of the law of attraction to a higher level. The Hot-Air-Balloon script works best when you listen to it before falling asleep.

To fall asleep while you have these positive golf images on your mind requires certain physiological changes. Your brain needs to start generating its own images and sensations as the first step to sleep. Also, before you fall asleep, there needs to be a very subtle temperature shift in your body. This happens when your core body temperature drops in comparison to that of your extremities.

In the upcoming self-hypnosis script, you will learn to produce these responses, thereby encouraging the onset of sleep to be well rested before your game the following day and to program your subconscious mind to align with the most beneficial outcome for your game.

Science is continually becoming more aware of the health benefits of good-quality sleep. Proper sleep helps us live longer, have a better functioning immune system to fight illness and disease, concentrate and remember better, have more stable moods, and have more mastery over our golf games! As you may have experienced, too little sleep can adversely affect your golf game. According to the Sleep Research Center at the University of California, Los Angeles, better sleep equals more energy, better focus, and more optimism. In my experience, I've witnessed that a better night's sleep leads to greater mastery over my mental game of golf.

You are encouraged to harness the same internal sensory systems that activate naturally when you fall asleep. This is known as your hypnogogic response, which always occurs when you fall asleep. You can bring this natural mechanism under your control.

Because your body and mind are most naturally suggestible and receptive in the minutes bookending your sleep, the ideal scenario is to be ready for bed, tucked into the covers with your earphones on (unless the person you share your bed with wants to listen along with you, in which case turn the volume up so both can hear).

As you listen to the audio recording or read it to yourself, don't worry if you begin to doze off before you get to the end. There are positive messages scattered throughout the self-hypnosis script that will begin the conditioning process at whatever point you stop listening.

Enjoy!

Hot-Air-Balloon Self-Hypnosis Script

Your Zone Golf Hypnosis Journey

Sit in a comfortable, quiet position, or recline with your head slightly elevated.

Uncross your arms and legs, and rest your hands, palms up, either by your sides or on your thighs.

Should an emergency arise at any time while in self-hypnosis, you can get up to take care of the situation simply by counting yourself up from zero to five. At five you will be wide awake, completely alert, and aware.

Close your eyes, and take three to five deep, relaxing breaths, signaling to your subconscious mind that you are now ready to enter into a deep state of self-hypnosis to radically improve your golf game.

Clench every muscle in your body tightly and hold for a count of ten: ten, nine, eight, seven, six, five, four, three, two, one, zero. Release.

Allow your body to feel the contrast of being tightly clenched and feeling completely relaxed.

Repeat this.

Clench your body once more, tightening every muscle and holding for a count of ten: ten, nine, eight, seven, six, five, four, three, two, one, zero. Release.

Breathe deeply as you relax totally and completely, allowing your body to feel completely relaxed.

Very good.

As you begin, take a few very deep breaths, and you may begin to notice certain parts of your body relaxing. Perhaps other parts are still a little tense. Just become aware of this, as your body continues to relax—the way your clothes feel on your body, the way the air feels as it gently brushes up against your face.

Notice your body being completely supported by the weight of the chair, couch, bed, or whatever it is that is holding you up.

As you read this, become aware of how good it feels to breathe in deeply and slowly, and to release completely. Feel your chest and stomach rise with each inhalation, and contract with each exhalation. Notice the release and the letting go that takes place now. With each breath that you exhale, you release all your cares of the day.

With each breath you breathe out, you let go of any and all tension that may linger in your body. And with each and every inhalation, you breathe in a sense of peace and relaxation.

Begin to count yourself down into a deeper state of relaxation. Start with five and move down to zero. At zero you will go deep asleep, a receptive state of focused relaxation. And with each count, you become more and more relaxed, and completely peaceful.

Begin with five, as you let go with each breath.

Four—all tension washes away.

Three—allow yourself to feel heavy in the chair or on whatever surface holds you up.

Two—let go more than before, as you prepare yourself to discover an inner resourcefulness that will improve the way you approach your golf game and relate to yourself as a golfer.

One—prepare to enter the Zone.

Zero—deep asleep. Each and every time you read or hear "deep asleep," you go quickly, soundly, and deeply to this depth or deeper for the purpose of entering the Zone and radically transforming your mental golf game.

Now that you are resting in deep asleep, you have access to your imagination. Give yourself permission to imagine that you are standing in the midst of your favorite golf course, and you have it all to yourself. It could be a golf course that you've played on before, one that you would like to play on, or a golf course that is made of your pure imagination. Get a sense of the beauty of the course, the color of the grass, the shade of blue of the sky. Become aware of any sounds you hear around you. Perhaps you hear the sounds of birds chirping. Become aware of the time of day it is. Feel the temperature of the air on your skin. Smell the fragrances around you, like the scent of freshly cut grass, honeysuckle, rosemary.

Out of the corner of your eye, at the far end of this golf course, envision a vibrant color that captures your attention. As this happens you become curious and begin to walk toward it. As you get closer, you begin to see that it is a hot-air balloon, painted bright red, green, blue, and yellow. Your curiosity gets stronger the closer you get, so you now begin to sprint toward this mysterious hot-air balloon.

You are now close enough you can touch it. You are surprised to see that your name is painted across the hot-air balloon in gigantic letters. You touch the wicker basket and look up to see this gigantic hot-air balloon with the letters of your name painted across it, and you realize that this is here just for you.

Your curiosity is piqued. You open the latch on the wicker basket and climb in. You feel a rush of excitement because you know you are going on an adventure, and you really want to see how this hot-air balloon flies. You notice that there are four sandbags inside the basket keeping the basket and the hot-air balloon tethered to the earth.

You pick up the first sandbag, the smallest one, and take a close up look at it and it says in big bold letters, "Doubt."

You feel the weight of this sandbag. You feel how it weighs you to earth, and you know that it represents all of your self-doubt, all the times you doubted whether you could improve your golf game. This bag contains all the times you didn't think you were good enough, all the cynicism you have about whether anything can help you improve. Like a magnet that pulls all particles of doubt from within you, feel all of your doubt being pulled from you and sticking to this heavy sandbag until all doubt is out of your mind and body. Take a couple of deep breaths, and when you feel that all the doubt is gone, with all your might drop the weight off over the edge of the basket. Thud!

Suddenly, the hot-air balloon lifts the basket you are in about ten feet off the ground, and you feel lighter, having removed the excess weight of your self-doubt. Take a breath to feel how refreshing the absence of self-doubt is.

Now, pick up the second weight, which in big, bold letters says, "Ego." It is a heavier weight than the previous one. Immediately, you begin to feel the detrimental aspects of your ego: all the times you worried about what other people would think of you, all the times you didn't let yourself be honest or authentic because you were caught up in how people (even strangers) might judge you. Begin to get a sense of how this has adversely affected your golf game. Contemplate all the mental noise, the inner chatter. Now suddenly, like a huge magnet, the weight begins to pull to it all the shards of ego that you are willing to give up. Feel all of the shame and worry, all the embarrassment, comparisons, and despair, being sucked out of you. Take three deep breaths and allow any lingering particles of your ego to be expelled from you and attached to this heavy weight. When you feel ready, and all the ego that you no longer wish to carry into your golf game is all gone, take a deep breath as you use all your might to toss the heavy weight over the edge of the basket. Let it drop and hear the thud as it hits the ground.

With that heavy weight gone, your hot-air balloon is free to lift up 70 feet higher into the air. Feel the levity and the lightness of being as you lift higher and higher into the air, feeling free without that constricting ego there to inhibit you. Take a deep breath and feel the relief.

Now that you've stabilized at eighty feet in the air, you have a desire to explore how much further you can travel. Take a look on the floor by your feet. There is another heavy sandbag. As you lift it up, you can tell that this one is the heaviest so far. As you lift it up closer to your face, you see in big, bold letters "your past."

As you look at this heavy weight, begin to notice all the ways in which your past informs your present moment. Note that your past identity as a person and as a golfer is the constant benchmark for the progress you try to make every day, but it is a heavy weight. As much as you cherish your memories and honor your history, right now you realize that you are not your past and that, by clinging to your past, you weaken your golf game; you ensure that your progress is very slow. In this moment, you realize that if you are to succeed at becoming the best golfer you are truly capable of becoming, you must let go of the past as a reference point for who you truly are. You might notice resistance to letting go of this one; of all the weights so far, this is the heaviest. But you realize that you are not losing your past, just simply loosening its grip on you so that you can create your present and your future according to your desire, not your predictable history, which really has no bearing on what is possible for you.

And now, like a high-powered magnet, pull all the shards of the past from you that stand in your way of becoming the best golfer you are capable of becoming. Take some deep breaths as you feel these shards of the past being pulled from your mind, from your body—all the disempowering beliefs, all the limiting notions.

When you feel that they are all pulled out, take a look at the heavy weight with all the shards attached to it. When you are ready, take a deep breath and conjure all your strength as you drop this weight over the side of the basket and hear a thud.

You feel a wave of immediate relief and freedom from having that heavy weight removed from you. Now your hot-air balloon lifts up an additional 50 feet higher. It feels wonderful, expansive, yet completely safe and secure, because you are now free from your past, from your ego, and from your self-doubt.

Once you acclimate to this new height and see the world from a perspective that's even higher, feel the expansiveness of your newfound vision and begin to imagine the impact this freedom will have on your golf game.

As soon as you become comfortable here at this new elevation of 130 feet, you get a bit restless, because you know that there is still one thing holding you back from complete freedom as a golfer and as a human. With determination you lift up the last weight, and you feel that it is by far the heaviest one yet. It takes all your strength to hold it up so that you can read "fear" in big, bold letters.

Immediately, you begin to notice that there are still vestiges of fear in your mind and body. You might rationalize that some of the fear you maintain keeps you alive, but the fear in this sandbag is not discernment and wisdom; the fear in this sandbag is the weight of all the fear that holds you back and that keeps you from enjoying the life of freedom, peacefulness, and ease that you truly deserve. The fear in this sandbag is the fear that creates yips and that causes you anxiety in the middle of the night—it is the fear that keeps you from living in the Zone on and off the golf course.

Take three deep breaths and begin to feel these pockets of fear dislodging and being pulled out of you. Feel those layers of heaviness that fear creates being removed from you. As this happens, begin to notice that you are beginning to look and feel younger, more agile, freer—more yourself than ever before!

As you are releasing the last bits of fear, especially those last stubborn parts that want to hide out and hold on, feel the weight of the sandbag in your hands. When you are ready to release this burden, take a deep breath, lift it over the edge of the basket, and let it drop all the way to the ground. Listen for the loud thud that lets you know it is gone! As this fear sandbag hits the ground, all those weights enrich the soil on the golf course, creating the greenest grass and the most vivid flower garden you've ever seen.

And now with fear removed from your body and mind, you are free to direct your hot-air balloon to go as high as you would like, and in whichever direction, at whatever speed gives you the greatest pleasure.

Take a couple of deep breaths to anchor this feeling of being free of doubt, free of ego, free of your past reference points that would tell you what your limitations are, and free from fear. You are free to explore the vastness of who you are and what you are capable of. Travel here by the power of your mind wherever you want to go, feeling safe, secure, and in control. (Allow a few minutes of silence.)

And now as you are floating here, create a touchstone of this experience as a way to describe this new you so that you can draw from this experience later in your golf game. To help you describe the new you, answer the following questions (I suggest that you write down your answers):

- What is the primary emotional feeling I am present to right now (e.g., freedom, relief, expansiveness, love, excitement, peacefulness, aliveness)?
- What is the primary physical feeling that I feel now (e.g., tingling, lightness, floating)?
- If this feeling had a sound, what would it be (e.g., silence, angelic choir, a sigh, a favorite song)?
- If it had a smell, what would it be (e.g., freshly cut grass, the ocean, flowers, fresh-baked cookies)?
- If it had a taste, what would it be (e.g., mint, chocolate, cookies, clean air)?
- If it had a voice, what would it say (e.g., "You are magnificent," "Just let go," "This is who you really are")?

As you connect with all the aspects of your touchstone, begin to get a sense of the way in which this newfound energy organizes itself to affect your golf game. (Allow a few moments of silence.)

Begin to feel an excitement in anticipation of your next golf game, and get a sense of the way that you will play. Notice what is different about the way you play now compared to the way you used to play. Think about the main differences. (Allow a few moments of silence.)

Take three deep breaths as you lock in this touchstone: its feeling, sound, scent, taste, words. When you are ready, by the power of your mind, begin to gently descend in your hot-air balloon, gracefully, slowly down to the ground, at exactly the pace you want.

As soon as you land and step out of the basket, you see that there are a set of clubs and a ball on the grass waiting for you.

You excitedly choose a club. Just before you tee off, take a deep breath, calling to mind your touchstone. Then take one more deep breath as you focus on where you want the ball to go, and swing. Feel the wonderful sensation of the ball connecting with the club as your body and mind are in perfect alignment.

You can continue to imagine yourself golfing eighteen holes like this, or you can climb back in your hot-air balloon and continue exploring. It is your hot-air balloon, after all, and you can use it any time you'd like, any time you need a higher view, any time you want to lighten your load, or any time you want a refreshed perspective on who you are without doubt, ego, your past, and fear.

In fact, the more often you repeat this experience, the stronger your reference point will be of this free, powerful, masterful golfer. Now go deep asleep, quickly soundly, and deeply to this depth or deeper, a bit deeper than before.

Now, you are taking this experience deep inside your subconscious mind, to the hard drive of your mind's computer, the place that controls your choices, decisions, and reference point on the golf course. As you sleep, this positive inner reference point of how to see and be yourself on the golf course, in your golf game, any time, anywhere, will saturate your subconscious mind.

If you are going to sleep now, continue to rest, deeper and deeper with each breath. Give thanks to yourself for all that you have just experienced, and drift deeper now to deep asleep. You know that when you awaken in the morning, you will be well rested, alert, aware, and you'll feel great. But for now, go deep asleep, even deeper than before.

System Upgrade While You Sleep

Man's mind, once stretched by a new idea, never regains its original dimension.

—Oliver Wendell Holmes

You would never think today of using an old computer from the early 1980s. It wouldn't work—it's out of date and it would not be able to perform the tasks you need. We laugh when we see pictures of those huge, bulky computers. They seemed so high-tech back then, but today they are obsolete, dinosaurs from the distant past.

From time to time, all of us improve our computers. We upgrade the system to get that old computer in line with today's world.

Our thoughts work in the same way.

Most of us use the same fight-or-flight patterns that kept us alive many moons ago but now simply keep us from living at the highest, most exalted level of which we are capable.

For the sake of argument, to become the best golfer you can be, much less to play in the Zone, you need a system upgrade. Let's take a look at what that means. In the old system, a missed shot was cause for alarm, inner ridicule, and being plagued with defeat and failure. This response, for most people, is so hardwired that it happens within a millisecond of missing the shot. Before you know it, you are throwing yourself down on the green, red faced and having a tantrum (OK, maybe you just want to do that).

This outdated operating system, which most of us are still using, keeps us from ever wanting to make a mistake because of the enormous pain attached to doing so. This makes for a pretty miserable game of golf, when you consider that the entire game is about mistake management and course correction.

But with a system upgrade, the rules are completely different, even opposite. The name of the game with the new upgrade is to make as many mistakes as possible, with complete freedom and a sense of humor.

"What?!" you must be thinking. "She's crazy! That'll never work!"

Well, dare I ask, at the risk of sounding like Dr. Phil, "How's your retro system working for ya?"

With the new system upgrade, you know that when you miss a shot or if a shot doesn't go exactly to the target you set out to hit, this is actually a good thing. It is good because you are learning, just as a baby who must make thousands of mistakes to perfect the art of walking, eating, and talking. Each mistake you make brings you one quantum leap closer to becoming a better golfer.

Try the Freedom Technique Exercise (If You Dare!)

Go out on the golf course and for one round (at least three holes), hit the ball as wildly as possible. Change the rules of the game to whoever gets the highest score wins. I know this is making you squeamish. You might think, "Are you talking to me?"

Yes, I am talking to you. When you give yourself permission to make mistakes, you will find that something very strange begins to happen. You won't make as many mistakes as you thought you would. When you rigidly grasp for perfection, you make the biggest goofs, take yourself way too seriously, and suffer horribly.

But when you try to make mistakes, you give yourself the freedom and flexibility to discover how talented you actually are. When I ask golfers to tell me about their best game, it is always when they are the most relaxed, not keeping score, and enjoying the moment-by-moment experience.

Once you get accustomed to this system upgrade, you will laugh when you think back on how you used to react when you missed a shot, the way you shuddered in shame when your ball rolled into the bunker, the way your shoulders used to tighten up, the way you would curse under your breath, the mental lashings with which you used to abuse yourself.

You will know that your system upgrade has been properly installed when missed shots and self-berating become laughable. At this point, you will be operating in a completely different matrix where the former rules no longer apply, and you will be golfing better than you ever have.

Another way to upgrade your system is to think of every mistake as cause for celebration, because mistakes contain valuable lessons that will lead you to be better than you are right now. In fact, you can look forward to making mistakes, because you know that if you do not make hundreds of them a day, then you are not improving in a quantum way.

You now have the complete freedom to make mistakes: the more the merrier, because you know that this is actually the fast track to rapid learning and growing, and this is one of the easiest ways to access the Zone.

If your ego, as a remnant from your old system, has a slip and sends an error code, telling you that it is not OK to make a mistake, then the only appropriate response is to hit the delete key on the computer in your mind and allow yourself to laugh at the humor of it all.

Preparing for the System-Upgrade Self-Hypnosis Script

The mind craves "normal," a state called homeostasis in which you are in balance with your view of self, others, and the world. This is why we typically reject anything too bad or too good: we want to filter into our experience only that which reinforces our view of the world.

At first blush, when you see in your mind's eye how well you play with your new system upgrade, your conscious mind (12 percent of your mind's power) might initially reject it as unrealistic or too good to be true, and certainly not normal. However, when you sleep on it, you'll ease yourself into this newer, better way of playing and being. By the time you wake up in the morning, what was startling and hard to believe the night before will have become your new conditioned state of normal. This illustrates the power of dreamwork, sleep, and your subconscious mind.

The following self-hypnosis session is meant for you to read just as you drift off to sleep the night before a game, to assist your subconscious mind to absorb and integrate your system upgrade as you sleep deeply.

Enjoy!

System-Upgrade Self-Hypnosis Script

Your Zone Golf Hypnosis Journey

Sit in a comfortable, quiet position, or recline with your head slightly elevated.

Uncross your arms and legs, and rest your hands, palms up, either by your sides or on your thighs.

Should an emergency arise at any time while in self-hypnosis, you can get up to take care of the situation simply by counting yourself up from zero to five. At five you will be wide awake, completely alert, and aware.

Lie down in a comfortable position, ideally in your bed as you prepare for sleep. Close your eyes.

As you lie down to sleep, feel a progressive relaxation move throughout your body as you begin to deeply relax.

Imagine that a very comfortable sensation is moving down through the crown of your head, gently relaxing your eyes, emptying out all the mental chatter and commentary from the day you have just had. With each breath you are emptying out and letting go, becoming lighter and lighter, becoming weightless, comfortable, and deeply relaxed.

Feel the warmth and relaxation moving down into your shoulders, down into your hands and wrists, allowing any residual tension, doubt, or fear to empty out through your fingertips. Take a deep breath to allow this deep release.

Move the relaxation down through your chest, allowing it to fill up with spaciousness, clear out any hardness around your heart, any defenses, any limits to how great you think you are capable of being.

You are now opening up completely to receive the system upgrade that will have you playing at your personal best, as the natural golfing genius that you truly are. Take another deep breath and feel flooded with grace, ease, and a wonderful feeling about your golf game tomorrow.

Move deeper down into your stomach area, through your lower back, and feel the seamless synergy of your muscles, your mind, your body, and your spirit preparing you for your next game. You are preparing yourself to sleep deeply and easily, to allow your deep subconscious to support you with clear directives about you playing from now on at your ultimate and highest capacity.

Drift down deeper into your pelvic area, and feel your groin muscles relaxing and letting go and finding their synchronicity with the rest of your power centers.

Easily and gracefully move this relaxation down through your thighs and buttocks. Notice a warm light make its way down through your bones, sinews, and veins, allowing you to become lighter still—down into your knees, calves, ankles, and feet. You feeling completely light.

As you rest in this relaxation, imagine that you are standing on top of a green hill on your favorite golf course on a crisp morning. Notice the light shining behind you, illuminating you, warming you, and encircling you.

As you stand atop this hill, you are filled with confidence. In fact, you are the embodiment of your highest self: glowing and standing in your power. You feel and access your inner strength and power to move through you, illuminating you from the inside out until you become as bright as the sun.

As you take each of the next five steps down this hill, you are receiving your new system upgrade that enables you to release the chains of perfectionism from the past, allowing you to expand into greater freedom and joy, enabling your natural golf genius to be revealed without constraint with each step you take.

Five—you begin to move down the hill, taking a step with your left foot, smelling the freshly cut grass, feeling the warmth of the sun on your back and shoulders. You begin to feel a change taking place within your mind and body.

Four—as you drift down the hill, you are feeling connected with the new, inspired information that is replacing the old, fear-based system easily and effortlessly. You may notice a tingling sensation as this change takes place.

Three—as you are drifting farther down, your breathing, deep and relaxed, is in rhythm with your heartbeat, slow and steady. You feel weightless.

Two—move gracefully down. As you near the bottom of the hill, you are preparing to let go entirely and you feel that the upgrade is almost complete.

One—as you arrive at the bottom of the hill, you are feeling more peaceful and relaxed.

Zero—deep asleep. Each and every time you hear or read "deep asleep," you will go quickly, soundly, and deeply to this depth or deeper for the purpose of upgrading your ability to golf in the Zone and for personal improvement. Deep asleep.

As you are at the bottom of the hill, you feel a very pleasant sense of spaciousness within you, combined with a wonderful, heightened sense of focus. It is like a waterfall that sparkles as it washes down through the crown of your head, down, down, down through your entire being. This waterfall is washing you clean of the reference points from your old system and completely renewing you, cell by cell, atom by atom, thought by thought. Rest here in the silence, as you are becoming integrated into this new, heightened system of thought. (Allow a few minutes of silence.)

Now begin to walk across the golf course, feeling the change, feeling the upgrade. When you are ready, choose a hole to begin at. Perhaps this will be one of the most difficult holes to play. You notice that your bag of clubs is right there. You place the ball on the tee, and take a couple of practice swings. As you do, you take a deep breath, reminding yourself of your system upgrade. As you breathe, you remember that you have the freedom to play without constraints, without perfectionism, in a way that allows your natural genius to emerge. A smile spreads across your face, signaling to your subconscious mind that you are in an expanded state of complete freedom. With this, see yourself swing and hit the ball. Notice that the ball goes exactly where you want it to go even though you were relaxed and having fun.

Now, hit the ball recklessly. Even as you are goofing around, your natural genius takes over and manages to get the ball near where you want it to go.

In your mind's eye, see and feel yourself playing a few more holes, so that you can get used to the way you play with this system upgrade. (Allow a few minutes of silence.)

Begin to notice how you are different now from the way you used to play with your old operating system.

Now, with the next few deep breaths, project yourself into the future, a year from now. Imagine that you have continually kept up with the upgrades to your system and are even better than you are now. Take a few moments to breathe this in.

What are you like a year from now, having improved in a quantum way? Are you even better than you see yourself being now?

How does this feel? How does this change look? Examine the nuances of the way your system upgrades look and feel a year from now.

As you sleep tonight, you will be absorbing these system upgrades deep into every aspect of your being. Your subconscious mind cannot discern between that which you vividly imagine and that which is real, so as you sleep tonight and dream the dreams of this system upgrade, you will accelerate and amplify its effectiveness. And when you awaken tomorrow morning, you will begin to feel and see a change. Pay close attention to what the changes are. Remember that where attention goes, energy flows and results show.

Deep asleep. Signal to your subconscious mind that you are going deep asleep, quickly, soundly, and deeply to this depth or deeper.

And now with the next deep breaths, prepare for a deep, restful sleep. And as you do, know that your system upgrade is reorganizing your inner reference points. When you awaken in the morning, you will feel refreshed and rejuvenated, and you will notice right away the improvement in your game and in your overall well-being. Deep asleep. Drift deeper than ever before.

Secret Takeaways

- What if you could allow one of your greatest natural assets, your dream time, to actually work for you?
- When you are asleep, you are in the most vulnerable, suggestible state of being. This is truly magic time, when 88 percent of your mind's power is truly accessible.
- All affirmations are not created equal.
- Your body and mind are most naturally suggestible and receptive in the minutes that bookend your sleep.
- If you do not make many mistakes in a day, then you are not improving in a quantum way.

ZONE SWEET ZONE

Put your passion in action

Great news: We are designed to live in the Zone with the strong foundation of a healthy physical body and mental body.

—*John Gray, PhD*

Secret Synopsis

When you flip your passion switch, in effect, you are feeding your brain dopamine and serotonin, which stabilizes your ideal mental and emotional states. You will realize that with the strong foundation of a healthy physical and mental body, you can easily make the Zone home sweet home, or rather Zone sweet Zone.

Mind, Body, and Spirit

Golf is a recreation that requires infinite patience and eternal optimism.

—*Carl Hiaasen*

The spirit inspires, the mind directs, the heart responds, and the body sustains.

—*John Gray*

Having a healthy brain, one that is habitually oriented toward passion and being in the Zone, is the foundation for all the positive changes we wish to make on and off the golf course.

Let's talk a little about the brain. According to Daniel Amen, PhD, a brain-scan specialist from Amen Clinic in California, we have more links in our brain than we have stars in the galaxy. Try wrapping your head around the fact that there are 100,000 neurons in a piece of brain tissue the size of a single grain of sand. With almost 100 billion of these neurons in our head, our brain is more complex than most of us can fathom.

We humans comprise mind, body, and spirit. What affects one affects the other. For example, you can endeavor to think all the right Zone thoughts on the golf course, but if you do not eat healthy food or get adequate rest, then you will no doubt struggle with your ability to keep your mind in the Zone. However, when you position yourself for success by eating healthy food, getting proper rest, enjoying healthy relationships, and practicing the self-hypnosis sessions laid out in this book, then you are painting yourself into a Zone corner—it will be nearly impossible to not be in the Zone.

The Zone is natural, the way you were meant to function. If you ensure that you are doing all the right things (e.g., eating a balanced breakfast instead of three doughnuts on the way to the golf course), then your body will produce the correct balance of hormones to bring you to the Zone. All of this will affect your mind, the way you think, the way you play golf.

Let's dissect the Zone from a biochemical perspective. According to John Gray, PhD (author of *The Mars & Venus Diet & Exercise Solution-Book*), to operate at peak performance, we need a balance of dopamine and serotonin. Dopamine is a chemical in the brain that pumps us up and helps us take on the day. Serotonin is a brain chemical that relaxes us and helps us remember that all is well. Both dopamine and serotonin are stimulated by the thoughts we think and the foods we eat.

When your dopamine and serotonin levels are out of balance, it is hard for you to focus. You have little concentration, an easy trigger, and scarcely the patience to line up your shots correctly. Without a balanced brain, it would be very difficult to swing your club and expect the ball to go straight toward your target. However, when your dopamine and serotonin levels are balanced, you have the heightened ability to focus on your shot; the insight to choose the right club; and the patience to make sure your mind, body, and spirit are aligned before you make contact with the ball.

You can flip your "passion switch" to stimulate your brain with dopamine and serotonin, thus elevating you quickly and steadily to the place that is your birthright: the Zone.

Preparing for the Passion Self-Hypnosis Script

What lies behind us and what lies before us are tiny matters compared to what lies within us.

—Ralph Waldo Emerson

Consider for a moment how you rate yourself as a golfer. On a scale from one to ten, how good of a golfer are you? Do you rate yourself a two and think that you have a fairway to go before you are where you think you should be? Or do you rate yourself an eight because you are already good but would like to improve ever so slightly to become your absolute best?

Now consider for a moment what a ten feels like. Take a few deep breaths, and imagine that you've fast-forwarded the movie of your life to the scene where you are exactly where you would most like to be as a golfer. Now stay here, breathing, feeling the sensation, the joy, the electricity, and the focus, of being your personal best.

Passion feeds the creation of dopamine and serotonin in your brain (dopamine pumps us up and serotonin chills us out), elevating you and stabilizing you in the place that is truly most natural for you. This next script is intended to help you to create and anchor a passionate reference point for yourself.

Enjoy your journey.

Passion Self-Hypnosis Script

Your Zone Golf Hypnosis Journey

Sit in a comfortable, quiet position, or recline with your head slightly elevated.

Uncross your arms and legs, and rest your hands, palms up, either by your sides or on your thighs.

Should an emergency arise at any time while in self-hypnosis, you can get up to take care of the situation simply by counting yourself up from zero to five. At five you will be wide awake, completely alert, and aware.

To prepare for your journey into passion, close the door to the outside world, recline in a comfortable position, uncross your legs and arms, place your palms face up in an open and receptive position, and begin taking some deep breaths. Imagine with each exhalation that you are setting your body temple free from all negativity, fear, apprehension, doubt, worry, separation—all preconceived ideas and disempowering beliefs about what you think passion is and how it relates to your golf game.

Now take a deep breath, and feel as though you are detaching from all that weighs you down or intrudes on your being totally connected to passion. And with each deep inhalation, begin to breathe in a golden light, or your favorite color, a color that represents passion to you. Is it purple, gold, blue, red, magenta, or white shimmering light? What color represents passion to you?

Feel this light travel throughout your entire body, relaxing and revitalizing you with each breath you take. Feel the color of passion traveling through the crown of your head, opening your third eye (the psychic center in the lower region of your forehead, between your two eyes), gently moving down your throat, shoulders, your chest, your arms, stomach, abdomen, lower back, pelvis, thighs, legs. It tingles down through the tips of your toes, and you feel your entire body filled with the energy of passion.

Imagine that you are standing atop a beautiful staircase that has five steps. See yourself completely luminous. You are your highest, most passionate self, overflowing with connection to the highest light of your being. Your power, magnetism, enthusiasm, and joy are a magnet for success, great opportunities, and wonderful people to gravitate toward you.

See yourself standing tall, ten feet tall, a loving, generous, powerful, successful, passionate giant, as you begin to make your way down the stairs. With each step you take and each breath, you are growing taller and stronger in your passion. You are becoming more deeply identified with this image of your most passionate self in your subconscious mind, and this image becomes your internal reference point.

Now, as you prepare to take your first step down the staircase, hold on to the handrail with your left hand and begin counting backward from five to zero. Each step takes you deeper and deeper into relaxation. You become more and more suggestible to the positive suggestions, and at zero, you will go deep asleep.

Five—take your first step down the staircase, taking a deep breath, deepening the suggestion of you being the embodiment of passion in your subconscious mind.

Four—you are now expanding in your passion reference point.

Three—you are becoming more relaxed but focused on your essence of success and passion building within you.

Two—as you engage with your passion, it feels so natural to you now, so ordinary, and so wonderful. Any old feelings of apathy, heaviness, doubt, and fear about your golf game are becoming a distant memory, something that you can laugh at as those memories become hazy and faded in your mind.

One—you are feeling so connected to your passion as you travel deeper and deeper and see at the bottom of the staircase a very comfortable bed, with the softest, most luxurious cushions you could ever imagine. You are about to fall into this bed.

Zero—deep asleep. You fall deeply and comfortably into this cushiony bed. Every time you hear or read "deep asleep," you fall quickly soundly and deeply to this depth or deeper, and your connection to your passion for being alive begins to build and strengthen with each breath you take.

Place your left index finger and thumb together and, as you do, silently say the word *passion* to yourself. This is your anchor to help you to connect with your unique expression of passion.

Now allow yourself to recall a memory of a time in your past, a pinnacle moment when you felt totally connected to passion. It may be golf related or it may not have anything to do with golf—it does not matter. Take your time to recall this passionate moment. It can be a moment from your recent past or a time from your youth. Choose one moment now.

Take a snapshot of that moment now. Freeze the moment in time.

Where were you?

Who were you with?

What time of day or night was it?

Allow yourself to be specific about what you see around you, the colors and details, the temperature of the air on your skin, fragrances around you, the sounds, and any words that were being said. Most important, come inside the feeling tone of this experience and feel how passion feels in your body, emotionally and physically. What kind of thoughts do you think when you are feeling passionate? How do you feel about yourself? What is your perspective on life when you are feeling passionate?

From this position of heightened passion, what is your perspective of yourself as a golfer? What thoughts do you have about the game of golf? What insight do you have for yourself into ways you can improve in your particular game?

Now as you are luxuriating in the height of passion, take three deep breaths and allow the feeling to amplify. If passion had a color, what color would it be? Now paint your entire inner vision with this color, paint the golf course in your mind with this color, and paint your entire world with this color. Paint your past as a golfer with this color, and paint your future as a golfer with this color.

Feel the innate wisdom of passion and intelligence. Become aware of its guidance system, where it leads you, and how it can inform you.

Envision your path of passion as a golfer laid out in front of you like a vein of gold, leading you to your highest vision, your grandest destiny, your greatest success as a golfer.

Envision yourself following the promptings that passion inspires, leading you from glory to greater glory along your golden path of golf success. Envision yourself magnetizing wonderful people, support, magic, wealth, and success that you deserve in the Zone of your highest possibilities.

Now place your left index finger and thumb together and, as you do, silently say the word *passion* again to yourself. This is your anchor to help you to connect with this feeling of passion, any time and anywhere. Deep asleep. Go quickly, soundly, and deeply to this depth or deeper.

Give thanks for your willingness to grow and glow into the successful, passionate golfer that you came here to be. If you are listening to this as you drift off to sleep, know that starting now, your sleep will be deep and restful, allowing you to awaken in the morning feeling refreshed and invigorated.

Now count back up.

Zero—deep asleep.

One—you begin to walk back up the staircase, feeling physically alert. Recalling your anchor, press your index finger to your thumb and silently say the word *passion* to yourself. This anchor reactivates and deepens your connection to passion on and off the golf course, assisting you with greater focus, patience, and intuition in your golf game.

Two—move up the staircase, feeling emotionally calm and saying the word *passion* silently to yourself as you press your left index finger to your thumb.

Three—take a deep breath, knowing that all the positive suggestions have taken root deep in the soil of your mind. Prepare yourself for the following: something wonderful is about to happen to you.

Four—become aware of where you are, the air on your skin. Your fingers and toes begin to wiggle.

Five—you find yourself back up at the top of the staircase, feeling wide awake and noticing a passionate smile spreading across your face, maybe even a giggle. You might try not to smile, but it is hard not to when you feel excited, inspired, and passionate about your golf game.

Have a passionate day!

The Star You Are

Every single one of us can do things that no one else can do—can love things that no one else can love. We are like violins. We can be used for doorstops, or we can make music. You know what to do.

—*Barbara Sher*

A star is who you are, beneath the cloak of your ego. When you can truly let go and dust off the cobwebs of self-importance and self-doubt, you will find a luminous treasure of your own inner genius.

One of the things that keeps most people from being in league with their star essence (and thus their most passionate expression) is a limited perspective of who they are. With this limited perspective comes stress, feelings of inadequacy, even a downward spiral of depression. When people have a paradigm shift from seeing themselves as disenfranchised beings to suddenly feeling worthy of their full inheritance of the goodness of life that is available to them, then they begin to allow happiness, joy, even passion to express itself in them, even as they golf. When you get out of your own way, far enough to let your natural radiance shine, you will be hard pressed not to be excited, not to feel really good, not to feel passionate (even when you drive the ball into a sand trap). This consistent feeling of well-being has a great deal to do with mastering the mental game and your ability to remain in the Zone.

There are many pathways to the Zone, several of which we've explored in this book. The Zone Golf star process is a way for you to quickly and easily step out of the mental chaos, frustration, and confusion that can cause clamor between your ears on the golf course and to step into that space of grace, the Zone, in which you are most likely to play at your very best, like the star that you are, at any given moment.

Star is an acronym for surrender, thanks, allow, and release.

When people are golfing in the space that we refer to as the Zone, they report feeling that it was not them doing the swinging or putting but that it was as if their ordinary self had stepped aside and something higher had stepped in and taken over. Some people report feeling used, as if their body was an instrument occupied by a higher, more graceful and skilled energy that was channeling through them.

In all cases, the golfers I've worked with and interacted with have said that being in the Zone is the goal. If the Zone could be bottled, it would be the hottest thing on the market—everyone would buy stock in it and become millionaires overnight. But one complaint that seems universal among golfers is that, as exhilarating as being in the Zone is, it is equally as frustrating being on the outside looking in.

I've found that there are several things that are under your control that can make you a receptive space for the Zone.

Becoming the Star You Are

Aim at the stars, and you may hit the top of the gatepost; but aim at the ground and you will hit the ground. It is not to be supposed that any one will attain to the full realization of what he purposes, even when those purposes do not involve united action with others; he will fall short; he will in some measure be overcome by contending or inert opposition. But something he will attain, if he continues to aim high.

—Voltairine De Cleyre

When you reach for a vision higher than you normally think you can obtain, you elevate yourself to higher caliber thought vibrations. In so doing, you place yourself on par with the great thinkers, creators, and golfers who have gone before you.

In becoming the star you, I don't encourage you to have delusions of grandeur in which your head gets so big you can't fit through the door of the clubhouse. It is not about inflating your ego to think that you are above everyone else in the world and that you are the greatest golfer on the planet.

Becoming the star you are is actually the opposite of what you might think. It is an act of great humility, not egoism. To accept and explore the greatness within you may be the most humble thing you will ever do. For when you acquiesce to that which is higher, it is as if you say, "I admit that it is not me and my little ego that is running the show of my life; I am willing to accept the higher pattern of the universe to inform me, to golf through me, that I may be an instrument to inspire others to step into their greatness."

Some people recoil at the notion that there is a star within them. If you are twitching with discomfort right now, please allow me to clarify. You are special, just like everyone else. There is a divine spark in us all, something special, something radiant, something truly magnificent. For some, this gift makes itself apparent on the golf course. For others, it is apparent in business or in matters of the heart. In any case, your star essence is unique, and when you choose to engage it, its wisdom will communicate with you in such a way that all aspects of your life will bear fruit, including your golf game.

Remember that where attention goes, energy flows and results show. By simply placing your attention on your inner star qualities or at least becoming curious about them, you are flowing energy to it, and you will be able to reap results.

There is also this saying: "That which you love will reveal its secrets to you." If you take a few minutes a day and simply open your heart to delve into the star within you, it will reveal its secrets to you.

Preparing for the Star Self-Hypnosis Script

Only as high as I reach can I grow, only as far as I seek can I go, only as deep as I look can I see, only as much as I dream can I be.

—*Karen Ravn*

There is an element of mystery to the Zone, kind of like falling in love. You can't guarantee how love or the Zone will take place, but you can take certain steps to put yourself in the optimum position so that if the Zone does show up, it can easily find you. Follow this Zone Golf star process to place yourself in the optimum mental space to find Zone sweet Zone.

Each step of the following Star self-hypnosis script includes a question to ponder to help you gain a vision of the star golfer and human being you truly are.

Step 1: Surrender
What must I release?

Take five deep breaths, and imagine with each breath that you are releasing everything you know, every moment that has preceded the moment at hand. Surrender from holding any and all tension from your body, any blame, and any fear, doubt, worry, hurry—everything and anything that does not serve you in your ultimate state of peak performance. When in doubt about what to surrender, let go of everything. Allow your body to feel the weight of gravity, and feel your shoulders slump like a rag doll. Let the muscles in your jaws go slack, your heart rate to slow, and your breathing to relax. With your eyes closed, see either complete blackness or complete brightness, a blank canvas, an opportunity to begin anew.

Of all the stages, most people resist this one the most. There is an unconscious desire to hold on, even if it is painful, even if what we are holding on to does not serve us. On some level, we equate surrender with defeat, or even worse, with death. If we are hard workers, we see surrender like giving up, throwing in the towel, and that simply goes against our every grain. However, when we realize that surrender is akin to sacrifice, and that sacrifice is about giving up something lesser in favor of connecting with something greater within ourselves, our resistance subsides. In this context, surrender does not mean to lose anything of any inherent value but to make room for something better, greater, more useful to step in and take over.

Perhaps we believe, on an unconscious level, that the stress and strain we carry around are somehow good for us, productive, worthwhile. Why else would we work so hard to carry them around with us day in and day out?

I was recently at the airport and realized that I could not check one of the bags I had planned to check. Instead, I had to carry it on the plane with me. It was not a roller bag but a heavy bag with a handle. My gate was at the far end of the airport, and I had to lug this bag all the way across the airport for what seemed like miles. Once I arrived at my gate, red-faced, sweaty, and scowling, I realized that because this bag was so heavy, it took all my energy and attention just to heave it from point A to point B. I was unable to make eye contact with any of my fellow travelers. I was unable to enjoy my usual opportunity to window-shop. In short, I was unable to enjoy the journey. Once my heavy bags were set down (once I surrendered my baggage), I could breathe, I could look up and around and see that life was actually going on around me, I could smile and make eye contact, I could have conversations, I could appreciate and be aware of the world of activity taking place around me that I previously did not have the luxury to notice.

It is impossible to be attuned to the visual and auditory cues around you, much less your own inner wisdom, when you are heavy laden. Taking deep breaths, releasing and letting go, and surrendering before each hole on the golf course will allow the fog to lift and your natural luminosity to shine, thereby clearing the decks for all that would stand in the way of your being in the Zone.

Step 2: Thanks

Let us rise up and be thankful, for if we didn't learn a lot today, at least we learned a little, and if we didn't learn a little, at least we didn't get sick, and if we got sick, at least we didn't die; so, let us all be thankful.
—*Buddha*

What am I grateful for?

The quickest way to attune the mind with the heart is through the practice of gratitude. Many of us have become accustomed to neglecting praise and focusing on criticism because we have bought into the false notion that criticism will help us grow more quickly than praise will. Nothing could be further from the truth. A star cannot shine without the radiance that comes from well-earned and well-deserved thanks.

When you get in the habit of starting your day with praise (and at least recognition) for yourself, for all the things that you have done right, and all the wonderful people and events that have helped in your evolution as a person and as a golfer, then you are in league with even more things for which to be grateful. When you praise yourself for showing up on the golf course, connecting with the ball, trying something new, sinking a putt, and making progress toward the goals you are working on, then you feel that you are succeeding, and there is nothing that breeds success like success.

You might also consider giving thanks to all of those who keep up the golf course, to the elements for providing a haven in which you are able to enjoy the luxury of self-improvement. Give thanks for your golfing companions for making the game more lively and competitive and for enhancing the learning environment.

To educate yourself for the feeling of gratitude means to take nothing for granted, but to always seek out and value the kind that will stand behind the action. Nothing that is done for you is a matter of course. Everything originates in a will for the good, which is directed at you. Train yourself never to put off the word or action for the expression of gratitude.
—Albert Schweitzer

Once you begin to prime your gratitude pump, you will find that there is no end to the things for which you can be grateful. And this enhances and strengthens your ability to stay in grace. The word *grace* (and the Spanish word *gracias*) is derived from the Latin word *gratus*, which had meanings such as "pleasing," "beloved," "agreeable," and "favorable." Giving thanks is most certainly one of the most accessible, surest entry points to the Zone.

Step 3: Allow

What quality will I allow myself to embody?

To allow something means to give permission to do or be something.

In the Zone Golf program, *allow* means for you to allow the natural essence and qualities of who you are into your consciousness. In other words, to allow yourself to acknowledge and thus amplify those starlike qualities within you, those which are already there, in your life and on the golf course.

Nature abhors a vacuum. Because you have successfully released unwanted energy and placed yourself in a state of grace by becoming grateful, you now want to be mindful and aware of the energy you want to allow in.

If you released stress, for example, you might consider allowing in the quality of ease or grace or fluidity. If you released the quality of self-doubt, then you might want to replace that energy by allowing in self-confidence. If you released distraction, then you might want to allow in the quality of focus, clarity, or certainty. If you released awkwardness, then you might want to allow in the quality of grace or elegance that is already alive within you but perhaps waiting in the wings.

Or you might contemplate the outcome you most desire to inform the quality you want to allow. For example, if you desire to make those high-stake putts, then delicacy, grace, precision, or patience would serve you. However, if you want to be able to tee off with more direct-ness, then qualities to embody might include strength, power, focus, or alignment.

Rev. Michael Beckwith says, "You cannot have something you are not willing to become" in consciousness. To truly see and experience the full breadth of your quality, take three deep breaths and imagine that you are breathing life into that quality with you. As if you were a sponge, drink this quality into your cells, your pores, your bones, your thoughts, your mind, and your imagination.

Step 4: Release

How can I get out of my own way?

If you haven't guessed by now, the star formula is all about release. Begin with surrender and end with letting go, and if you don't have time to do all that is in between, then you will be well served by simply taking a moment to release, let go, and wipe the slate clean. When you let go, you are out of your own way, and the magic within you can express itself.

Is it any wonder that most people play their best round of golf when they aren't keeping score? Notice the magic that happens when you play after letting go, when you get out of your own way and simply enjoy the scenery and have a good time? You've done it before, so you can do it again—it begins and ends with letting go.

This particular stage of release is also about fully expressing yourself, releasing yourself to your full self-expression, taking a risk, daring to look stupid, and having fun. If you aren't enjoying yourself, then you have lost the point and forgotten that this is a game, not work. Give yourself the freedom you would give to a child who is learning, stretching, growing, and improving.

I'll bet that you have heard this saying: "Dance like no one is watching, sing like no one is listening, and love like you've never been hurt." I've taken creative license and adapted it for the game of golf: "Swing like no one is watching, praise yourself like you're the star you are (and no one is listening), and golf like you've never missed a putt!"

Zone Golf Star Self-Hypnosis Script

Your Zone Golf Hypnosis Journey

Sit in a comfortable, quiet position, or recline with your head slightly elevated.

Uncross your arms and legs, and rest your hands, palms up, either by your sides or on your thighs.

Should an emergency arise at any time while in self-hypnosis, you can get up to take care of the situation simply by counting yourself up from zero to five. At five you will be wide awake, completely alert, and aware.

Close your eyes and nod your head slightly, signaling to your subconscious mind that you are ready to enter a deep state of self-hypnosis to radically improve your golf game.

As you begin, take a few very deep breaths, and you may begin to notice certain parts of your body relaxing. Perhaps other parts are still a little tense. Just become aware of this, as your body continues to relax—the way your clothes feel on your body, the way the air feels as it gently brushes up against your face.

Notice your body being completely supported by the weight of the chair, couch, bed, or whatever it is that is holding you up.

As you read this, become aware of how good it feels to breathe in deeply and slowly, and to release completely. Feel your chest and stomach rise with each inhalation, and contract with each exhalation. Notice the release and the letting go that takes place now. With each breath that you exhale, you release all your cares of the day.

With each breath you breathe out, you let go of any and all tension that may linger in your body. And with each and every inhalation, you breathe in a sense of peace and relaxation.

Begin to count yourself down into a deeper state of relaxation. Start with five and move down to zero. At zero you will go deep asleep, a receptive state of focused relaxation. And with each count, you become more and more relaxed, and completely peaceful.

Begin with five, as you let go with each breath.

Four—all tension washes away.

Three—allow yourself to feel heavy in the chair or on whatever surface holds you up.

Two—let go more than before, as you prepare yourself to discover an inner resourcefulness that will improve the way you approach your golf game and relate to yourself as a golfer.

One—prepare to enter the Zone.

Zero—deep asleep. Each and every time you read or hear "deep asleep," you go quickly, soundly, and deeply to this depth or deeper for the purpose of entering the Zone and radically transforming your mental golf game.

As you take a deep breath, allow yourself to envision that you are looking up to the sky. There is a clear, wide-open space. Imagine that sky in your mind: wide and open, clean and clear.

Surrender to the emptiness, openness, and a wide-open space, an opportunity to begin anew. Take deep breaths, releasing and letting go, to instantly attune you to the Zone.

Rest here in this wide-open, surrendered place, and suddenly imagine that you see the first star in the night sky. The twinkling of this star triggers a feeling of gratitude for who you are, where you are in your life, for the fact that you are taking time out of your life to improve your mental game. Notice how gratitude elevates your mood and enhances your perception.

It's daylight now. See yourself on the golf course, having built your gratitude muscles, offering gratitude for everything (and I mean everything) that happens to you, from the shots you make to the shots you miss. Notice the way this attitude of gratitude allows you to maintain connection to the Zone.

Now that you are in this field of gratitude, it is easy for you to allow in a quality that represents the essence you desire to embody. If you are still not sure what quality you want to allow, then contemplate the outcome you most desire on the golf course and let that outcome inform you of the quality to connect with now.

Call on that quality now (maybe it is peace, strength, focus, passion, clarity, patience, improvement, or confidence). Allow yourself to activate and evoke it with each and every breath. Take three deep, "allowing" breaths now.

You cannot have something you are not willing to become. In other words, you must evoke that quality within you to become a vibrational match to the quality or circumstance you desire. In this way, it must manifest in your life. That is exactly what you are doing right now simply by aligning yourself, breath by breath, with your desired state of being.

Once you have identified the quality you most wish to embody, take three deep breaths as you imagine that you are inhaling your quality into you as well as activating its vibration within you. As if you are lighting a match and intensifying its aliveness within your cells, your pores, your bones, your marrow, your thoughts, your mind, and your imagination, until you feel completely on fire with this wonderful quality of your choosing.

Marinate inside the following questions:

- Who would I be if I truly allowed this quality to overtake me, to have its way with me?
- How would I talk? How would I walk? How would I putt? How would I swing?
- How would my golf game improve if I truly embodied this quality?
- How would I walk between shots?
- How would I react when I missed a shot?
- What would my self-talk consist of?
- How might my life change if I embodied this quality?

Now, allow yourself to step inside the feeling tone of this quality as you magnify the image in your mind's eye of you fully embodying this quality. Allow your imagination to create this vision, feeling tone, or experience to become ten times stronger, more brilliant, more alive in you than before.

And now allow it to become ten times stronger than that. Take deep breaths as you receive this feeling tone, as it becomes you. With this breath, the quality you chose is inoculating you from unwanted energy.

This feeling tone that you are allowing is becoming an anchor within you, a reference point from which you derive clarity, focus, guidance, direction, and well-being on and off the golf course.

Consider this quote from the novelist Carl Hiaasen: "Golf is a recreation that requires infinite patience and eternal optimism."

Infinite patience and eternal optimism, infinite patience and eternal optimism—breathe that in and allow it to take hold. This is not so difficult to behold when you are in the Zone, or Zone sweet Zone.

Now that you are allowing in your desired quality and are aware of your inherent oneness with all of life, it is time to simply release and let go, release and have fun, release and play to your heart's content. As you take these next few breaths, do so and connect with the feeling tone of freedom, the freedom that comes from letting go—freedom from fear of making a mistake, freedom from fear of looking stupid, freedom from the constraints of your perfection—and the freedom that comes from releasing.

You have already done all the training you can possibly do on the physical plane, practiced all the techniques, and with the mental skills you've been mastering, it is now time to let it all go and trust that it is all within you now. The only job left is to see how much you can let go. Can you release more than you thought you could? Can you release more deeply, further, completely, turning yourself inside out and letting go?

Take one more deep breath, and imagine that you are watching a movie of yourself playing golf up on a big screen, larger than life. There you are, the embodiment of the qualities you most desire, truly playing golf like the star you are. You are completely undistracted in the Zone. From the moment you first tee off, through every fairway shot and every putt. As you maneuver past obstacles and line up your shots all the way to your final putt, you are watching, allowing, and learning from this new and improved version of you. On the movie screen, see how the camera zooms in to see how you have improved. Allow yourself to see the slight adjustment of the position of your hands, the slight change in your posture, your musculature, even your internal thoughts. Begin to sense the specific ways in which you are improving simply because of your willingness to be the star you are because of this slight adjustment in your perspective. (Allow a few minutes of silence.)

Now that you are aware of the star you truly are, take three deep breaths to allow this recognition to become deeply entrenched within you. Allow it to anchor itself and to alter and reorganize your previous perception, to realign it to what you have always known and to who you have always been.

As you rest here in this highly pleasurable sensation, notice that those old negative thoughts of criticism, worry, or despair seem utterly ridiculous to you now. A giggle might even erupt within you, perhaps a grin or a full-blown laugh. You see how funny it is that you are so vast, brilliant, unique, and wonderful that you could even entertain such petty nuisances. Allow yourself to see the absurdity and even the hilarity in it all.

While you are in this feeling tone of humor, review each of the four steps of the star process: surrender, thanks, allow, and release.

Review the star process again while you lock it in: surrender, thanks, allow, and release.

Each and every time you look up in the night sky and see the stars, you will anchor your awareness of your star qualities on and off the golf course. And now go deep asleep, quickly, soundly, and deeply to this depth or deeper.

When you can truly let go and get out of your own way, the magic within you can express itself. At this point, the Zone ceases to be a desired destination and is a starting point: Zone sweet Zone.

Take three deep breaths and begin to count yourself up from zero to five.

Zero—surrender to deep asleep, going quickly, soundly, and deeply to this depth or deeper.

One—feel grateful for yourself, for the experience of becoming a better golfer, a better human being. Feel how wonderful it is to allow gratitude to flood your awareness.

Two—allow the star quality you chose earlier to once again fill you up to overflowing.

Three—awaken and release the breath as you feel yourself awakening.

Four—recall all that you have learned and received, and your star formula: surrender, thanks, allow, and release.

Five—you are wide awake. Remember to golf like no one is watching, praise yourself like no one is listening, and let yourself shine like the star you are.

Secret Takeaways

- The real test of being in the Zone is whether you can continue to keep your cool and feel great even when your ball goes into the water.

- When you are out of your own way, the magic in you can express itself, at which point the Zone no longer is the destination but a launching pad into a new world.
- It is an act of humility, not egoism, to accept and explore the greatness in you. It is the height of arrogance to stake your claim in the territory of your trembling mediocrity.
- That which you love will reveal its secrets to you.

CONGRATULATE AND CELEBRATE

Congratulate and celebrate yourself for completing the 28-day Zone Golf Program and for mastering the mental game of golf!

By now, you will no doubt have noticed a change not only in the way you play golf but also in the way that you live your life and feel about yourself.

The following is a list of the secret takeaways from each chapter. In other words, at the conclusion of your 28-day journey, you have learned the following:

Secret #1: Z-own It!

- First create your desired outcome in your mind then put your body to work to bring the goal into a realized state. The way we do any one thing will show us how we approach our entire life.
- If you invest your attention on your intention the high ROI will be reflected in your low scores.

- We don't get what we want; we get what we expect.
- No expectations are expectations of "no."
- Many people short-change their lifetime achievement potential by basing their worth on short-term high expectations.

Secret #2: Lose Your Mind and Win the Game

- If you've been in the Zone at least once in your life, you can repeat it.
- Staying in a relaxed state of being is 88 percent of being in the Zone.
- Being in the Zone is when you, the club, the ball, and the range are one; when all the things that used to distract you seem miles away; and when you are focused, relaxed, and alert.
- Hypnosis is one of the most direct routes to get into the Zone.

Secret #3: The Heart of the Matter

- Don't believe your own thoughts.
- Take a "you turn" to your heart.
- Your heart being coherent is the essential key in your ability to have an impact on your golf game, on your life, and on the world.

Secret #4: The *One* in *Zone*

- Deep internal peace is accessible to anyone at any time.
- You get more of what you focus on.

Secret #5: Zone In

- It is scientifically proven that music is one of the quickest ways to shift your state of mind and put you in the Zone.
- Because you are a unique human being, the music that alters your state of mind and puts you in the Zone is as one-of-a-kind as you are.

Secret #6: Zone Out

- There are no mistakes, only unwanted results.
- The practice of perfection makes perfect.
- Exaggerate your memories from your hall of fame to ten times their intensity to associate them more deeply with your golf game.
- You are the thief of your very own golfer's gold.
- You can look at survival as a science and thriving as an art.

Secret #7: Sleep Your Way to Success

- What if you could allow one of your greatest natural assets, your dream time, to actually work for you?
- When you are asleep, you are in the most vulnerable, suggestible state of being. This is truly magic time, when 88 percent of your mind's power is truly accessible.
- All affirmations are not created equal.
- According to Abraham-Hicks, "The Law of Attraction, without exception, every human being has the ability to transform any weakness or suffering into strength, power, perfect peace, health, and abundance."

- Your body and mind are most naturally suggestible and receptive in the minutes that bookend your sleep.
- If you do not make many mistakes in a day, then you are not improving in a quantum way.

Secret #8: Zone Sweet Zone

- The real test of being in the Zone is whether you can continue to keep your cool and feel great even when your ball goes into the water.
- When you are out of your own way, the magic in you can express itself, at which point the Zone no longer is the destination but a launching pad into a new world.
- It is an act of humility, not egoism, to accept and explore the greatness in you. It is the height of arrogance to stake your claim in the territory of your trembling mediocrity.
- That which you love will reveal its secrets to you.

If you have not only read this book but also listened to the accompanying audio programs and practiced the exercises on the golf course, then you have received 80 percent of what the Zone Golf Program has to offer you. To expand your experience of Zone Golf, share your insights with a friend, colleague, or golf buddy who is struggling with something that you have learned to master. Remember, you keep that which you give away.

There is no ceiling on the possibilities of the golfer (or the human being) you are capable of becoming. And what makes this particularly exciting is that you now own the tools that you can take with you into your next golf game, and every game after that—improving step by step, breath by breath, and shot by shot.

As Tiger Woods said, "No matter how good you get you can always get better…and that is the exciting part."

For additional hypnosis script downloads and other bonus information, please visit www.sourcebooks.com/extras/zonegolf.

ABOUT THE AUTHOR

Carl Studna

Kelly Sullivan Walden is a certified clinical hypnotherapist. For fifteen years, she has been helping clients access their core beliefs, drives, and desires through their subconscious mind, to assist them in healing past traumas and aligning future goals.

Kelly is the author of *I Had the Strangest Dream: The Dreamer's Dictionary for the 21st Century.* She is also the author of *Discover Your Inner Goddess Queen: An Inspirational Journey from Drama Queen to Goddess Queen.* Kelly is a regular guest on FOX News New York and REAL RADIO 94.3/101.7 FM, WZZR. Her specialty is empowering people to live the life of their dreams.

Kelly is also the creator of the Dream Project (www.dreamprojectun .org), a movement for global change that inspires schoolchildren to create solutions for the UN Millennium Development Goals (to combat poverty, hunger, disease, illiteracy, environmental degradation, and discrimination against women). Ten percent of all proceeds from *Zone Golf* will be given to the Dream Project.

Kelly was introduced to the concept of Zone Golf by her father, Frank Sullivan. "We would go play a round of golf to have some 'father-daughter' time. At the end of the day we would wonder where the time had gone…and realize that without knowing it, we had stumbled into the Zone."

When Kelly met Bill Fawcett, a marketing expert and avid golfer, he saw her as a golfer's secret weapon, and they decided to create a program to assist golfers in improving their game and their enjoyment level.

Kelly is the president of the Women's National Book Association (Los Angeles chapter), and she is a nongovernmental organization delegate to the United Nations. She shares her life with her husband, Dana, and dog, Woofie, living part-time in the hustle and bustle of Los Angeles and part-time in the serenity of a ranch in Santa Fe, New Mexico.

Please visit Kelly at www.zonegolfnow.com.